# LEARNING IN A DISRUPTIVE AGE

Developing sound digital learning strategies

Letitia van der Merwe
and Graham Wolfson

TALENT MANAGEMENT SERIES

# Endorsements

As we know the Learning and Development world is constantly faced with change. The challenges range from, responding to the way people learn, to deciding on new technology solutions used to deliver learning. This is a very necessary piece of work to help organisations navigate digital learning solutions for the L&D world in this – as per the title – Disruptive Age. Thank you, the timing for this book could not be more perfect. Brilliant..."

*Nazreen Abrahams – Digital Learning Design Specialist*

Addressing talent development in the age of disruption and information overload has increasingly become a challenge for organisations. We operate in a context where there are a number of assessment instruments highlighting development areas in individuals, yet few answers as to how to address these areas. This book helps with the answers to those emerging development questions by presenting a framework with regard to digital learning. It enhances understanding by positioning the "modern" learner and presents guidance on an integrated digital strategy that addresses not only learning and development, but other areas of the talent management process. Thus, a relevant, engaging and thought-provoking read yet simplistic and interactive.

*Dr Leigh Zwaan, Talent Management Executive*

In the world of shifting businesses to accommodate disruptions, learning has become a pivotal tool in the hands of those crafting the shift. I believe this book addresses a topical theme and will undoubtedly provide L&D practitioners with relevant and up-to-date thinking, approaches and concepts regarding learning in the digital age, specifically within the context of the 4th Industrial

Revolution. The value of the book lies in the fact that it provides useful and practical guidelines on how to develop and implement a digital learning strategy in this time of disruptive technological developments! Of particular note is the use of QR codes to link digitally to extended sources of learning , and in this way the authors successfully combine "old world" books with digital learning artefacts – ground-breaking work!

*Jacques Strydom – Business Shift Catalyst, Customer experience and talent development specialist*

Copyright © KR Publishing and Letitia van der Merwe and Graham Wolfson

All reasonable steps have been taken to ensure that the contents of this book do not, directly or indirectly, infringe any existing copyright of any third person and, further, that all quotations or extracts taken from any other publication or work have been appropriately acknowledged and referenced. The publisher, editors and printers take no responsibility for any copyright infringement committed by an author of this work.

Copyright subsists in this work. No part of this work may be reproduced in any form or by any means without the written consent of the publisher or the author.

While the publisher, editors and printers have taken all reasonable steps to ensure the accuracy of the contents of this work, they take no responsibility for any loss or damage suffered by any person as a result of that person relying on the information contained in this work.

All cases are for illustrative purposes only and the intent is not to evaluate the performance of an organisation.

First published in 2019.

ISBN: 978-1-86922-812-5 (Printed)
eISBN: 978-1-86922-813-2 (PDF ebook)

Published by KR Publishing
P O Box 3954
Randburg
2125
Republic of South Africa

Tel: (011) 706-6009
Fax: (011) 706-1127
E-mail: orders@knowres.co.za
Website: www.kr.co.za

Typesetting, layout and design: Cia Joubert, cia@knowres.co.za
Cover design: Marlene de'Lorme, marlene@knowres.co.za
Editing and proofreading: Valda Strauss, valda@global.co.za
Project management: Cia Joubert, cia@knowres.co.za
Icons: By Freepik, www.flaticon.com and www.onlinewebfonts.com/icon/561962

# Acknowledgements

This book is dedicated to the dreamers who have the courage to turn dreams into reality.

Our heartfelt gratitude and appreciation go to the following people:

- Our clients and partners who, through the years, were willing to experiment and sometimes even fail with us.
- Our colleagues at inavit iQ for being true ambassadors of turning dreams into reality.
- Knowledge Resources for making this dream of a book a reality.

# Table of Contents

| | |
|---|---|
| **About the authors** | iv |
| **About the contributors** | vi |
| **How to read this book** | viii |

**Chapter 1:** The past, the present and the future ..... 1

| | |
|---|---|
| Introduction | 1 |
|     The organisation as a machine | 2 |
|     How this has impacted our view of training | 3 |
|     Entering from the side stage: the agile organisation | 8 |
|     The being of agile | 9 |
|     The doing of agile | 9 |
| Learning and Development: The Present | 10 |
| The Future: The Emerging Paradigm | 12 |
| Summary | 14 |

**CHAPTER 2:** Making sense of the disruption ..... 15

| | |
|---|---|
| Introduction | 15 |
| Part A | 16 |
| The Periodic Table of the Digital Learning | 16 |
|     Infrastructure | 17 |
|     Applications and Tools | 24 |
|     **Content, Design Methodologies and Approaches** | 28 |
|     Digital Myths | 31 |
| Summary | 34 |
| Part B: Meet the modern learner | 35 |
|     **Meet the modern learner** | 35 |
|     **Key features of the modern learner** | 36 |
|     Multi-generational learning | 38 |
| Summary | 41 |

**CHAPTER 3:** Designing a Digital Learning Strategy 43

Introduction 43
A thinking framework 45
Industry and internal dynamics and the regulatory
    environment 46
    Unpacking the environment 47
Learning Philosophy and Strategy 48
    Defining the learning philosophy 49
    Formulating the strategic objectives 53
Architecture and Value Chain 54
    The digital learning value chain 55
    Team structure 58
Design, delivery and governance 59
    Learning design 59
    **Learning delivery** 61
    **Learning governance** 61
Measurement and business benefit realisation 63
Summary 64

**CHAPTER 4:** Implementing a Digital Learning Strategy 65

Introduction 65
The art of getting things done 67
Learning on-boarding and a digital adoption approach 68
    Considerations for implementation 68
Learning on-boarding and digital adoption: a Roadmap 73
    Understanding human motivation – why would people
        learn? 74
    Asking people to learn in a new way 75
Digital adoption 77
Summary 81

**CHAPTER 5:** Are Kirkpatrick and Phillips still relevant? 83

Introduction 83
    Modern trends in learning measurement 84

| | |
|---|---|
| Are Kirkpatrick and Phillips still relevant | 84 |
|    **It starts with why** | 86 |
| What should be measured – The Digital Learning Dashboard | 87 |
| How should it be measured – Learning Analytics and Tools | 91 |
|    Design the logical dashboard | 91 |
|    Examples of digital measures and metrics | 92 |
|    Design the physical dashboard or scorecard | 94 |
|    Measurement we can't control | 95 |
|    Negative effects of measurement | 97 |
| Summary | 98 |
| What should be reported on to whom and the decisions to be made – Learning Reporting Framework | 99 |
|    Reporting Framework: Information about the strategy execution | 102 |
|    Reporting Framework: Information about the learner and the learner experience | 103 |
|    Reporting Framework: Information about business impact | 104 |
|    **Creating a culture of measurement** | 104 |
|    **Storytelling with Data** | 105 |
| Summary | 105 |
| **References** | 107 |
| **Index** | 110 |

## About the Authors

**Dr Letitia van der Merwe** predominantly collaborates with clients in the area where employees support the achievement of specific outcomes that impact on business benefits to be delivered. In thinking about this interface, she is mindful, deliberate and specific about how adults learn in the workplace; why, what and how we develop people; how we measure their competence levels and making sure we see learning and development not as events, but as integrated processes.

Her areas of specific expertise include leadership and change, client centricity and project management. Her career encompasses experiences from a wide range of Leadership, Human Resources and Organisational Development projects and interventions in the private and public sector as well as in the world of consulting.

She is an industrial psychologist by profession and is the co-author of the book *Reshaping Leadership DNA* and lead author of the book *Building the Corporate Leadership Community*.

**Graham Wolfson** has spent a significant part of his career working in the field of learning and technology. He has been in the consulting business for more than 15 years, working predominantly on projects where virtual learning was selected as a mechanism to upskill the employee base. His interests lie in the way that people interact with technology and how it can best be utilised to make the most of its benefits while avoiding its pitfalls.

Graham has a BA Communications degree majoring in Industrial Psychology and Communications. He has experience in human resource development and training strategies focusing on electronic- and computer-based interventions. He worked in the UK for eight years for a company specialising in software development to service the Higher Education and private training provider market where he operated as a Project Manager and Instructional Designer. He also has extensive experience in the process of designing, building and implementing bespoke software systems focusing on the initial needs analysis, documentation of functional requirements, design and prototyping of user interfaces, managing development resources, testing, User Acceptance Testing, Usability Analysis and procedural documentation/virtual learning.

# About the Contributors

**Yolandi Haveman** holds a BPsych(Hons) in Psychology and MCom in Industrial Psychology from the University of Pretoria. She has been in the consulting business for more than ten years, specialising in areas such as business process design, organisation design, governance and management practices, organisation development, organisational change management and organisational performance & capacity management. She has also completed certification in Business Process Redesign and Improvement, and has been working on business and organisation architecture projects in both the public and private sectors, locally and internationally.

Supporting this work are specialised partners and associates who provide professional services in the fields of Operating and Commercial Model Design, and Technology Architecture/Solutions. She is accredited with the Health Professions Council of South Africa and has published two articles and a book chapter. Her work with client systems is strongly influenced by the Systems Theory, Principles of Requisite Organisation and the Business Motivation Model. Her passion is to ensure that organisations and work are efficiently (process and structure) designed to ensure that their human capital can be effectively tasked, managed and developed to perform.

**Marita Booysen** has extensive experience in the field of Learning and Development – combining logical and analytical skills with creative design, development and implementation of learning solutions. She has worked in various industries ranging from Education, Mining, Agricultural, Health and Safety, Academia and Manufacturing, to Financial.

Unlocking hidden potential is Marita's primary life force. She works with people to unlock their respective talents and gifts, and then assists them in finding ways to realise these talents.

Marita has a very good understanding of creative learning methodologies and instructional design, providing a solid foundation for the conceptualisation and development of bespoke learning solutions in the creation of learning experiences. She is passionate about new trends in learning technology and enjoys taking such solutions to the next level of blended learning.

She has co-authored and authored a few publications, with her latest publication being *Succeed in Economics*. She is a founding member of the Workplace Learning Hub, and has collaborated in drafting the Workplace Learning Standard for the South African Board of Personnel Practice (SABPP).

## How to read this book

To a certain extent it is rather ironic to write a book about digital learning. You would assume the book also needs to be "digital". In order to write a book more in line with our approach to digital learning we tried to incorporate a number of practices.

### QR Codes

You will find throughout the book a number of QR codes. These odd-looking, black-and-white, pixelated designs contain links to a number of other resources (e.g. books and videos) that you may find useful. Here are some tips on how to use a QR app to access the data you want.

First, you need a QR-code app and a smartphone or tablet equipped with a camera. When you launch your app of choice, you'll see that your phone's camera is activated, with an on-screen framing guide. Line up the camera on your device with the QR code you want to scan, and hold the device steady until the app can read the code in front of it. When the app has recognised the QR code, it will beep and launch your Web browser to take you to a designated URL.

### Templates

If you are interested in an electronic version of some of the templates we mention in the book you can email learning@inavitiQ.com with the book's ISBN number. We will provide you with an access code and link to the info.

### A Moment to Reflect, Guides and Checklist

This is a practical how-to book. In Chapters 3 and 5 we provided you with tools and a checklist that you can adapt and use to suit your needs. The book also provides you with places to reflect on your thinking and unique context.

# Chapter 1

## The past, the present and the future

> *"The ability to learn faster than your competitors may be the only sustainable competitive advantage."* – Arie de Geus

## Introduction

In 2013 Higher Education Minister Blade Nzimande said *"South Africa has spent R57-billion over the past 10 years through the Setas in various training programmes, but the country does not have much to show for this investment..."*[1]

There are a number of reasons for this. In our view one of the key reasons is that we have become so fixated on qualifications and credits that we failed to consider the entire learning and development landscape. We no longer think systemically about learning and development. We may provoke a bit of controversy here but we think we find ourselves in the middle of a learning and development system geared towards organisations functioning on business models more appropriate to the 70s and 80s. We haven't considered the implications for organisations of the 21st Century and that people and business leaders need to deal on a daily basis with complexities unheard and unknown of in the past.

Organisations are also rapidly changing the way they do things as well as the technology that they use to execute the demands of the environment. We are in the midst of the 4th Industrial Revolution (4IR) that, simplistically viewed, refers to new ways in which we familiarise ourselves about and use technology in our lives – on a personal level as well as in our organisations. Robotics, artificial intelligence (AI) and nanotechnology are just some of the examples of the 4IR.

Furthermore, the workplace environment is not always conducive to learning. Employees lack time to reflect on learning and failure is often punished. The latest LinkedIn Report[2] on learning in the workplace identifies the #1 challenge for talent development as getting employees to make time for learning. It seems that employees on average have about 24 minutes per week available for learning. This is further complicated by the fact that learning is seen by some as separate from working and as taking 'time out' from productive work.

However, despite our statements above, the purpose of this chapter is not to look at everything that has gone wrong or is wrong – but rather to explain how the traditional or classical paradigm of seeing organisations as machines has impacted on a rigid and inflexible approach to corporate training. We will unpack the new business paradigm that predominantly focuses on themes with regard to the agile organisation and build the case for the need for a new paradigm for training or, as we prefer to call it, learning and development.

The remainder of the book will unpack how to design, implement and measure the implementation of a digital learning strategy on the current and emerging paradigms of learning and development.

## The organisation as a machine

Unfortunately, the classical paradigm which sought to make organisations run like well-oiled machines, to a large extent still remains the basis of our modern management thinking and practices.

This mental model or approach has resulted in:

- Leadership being seen to be effective only when it is founded upon a well-defined hierarchy of authority. Discipline is defined and interpreted by the leader, resulting in a select few that:
    - Are regarded as being superior and
    - Should have the answers to all our problems.
- Systems and process being seen as something to reduce uncertainty and increase predictability. While we are not arguing against the need to sometimes reduce complexity, these systems made organisations slow. They result in compliance and a model where the checker checks the checker, checks the checker.
- A bureaucratic model built on unquestioning loyalty and resulting in paternalism and cultures in organisations equivalent to that of a "family".

What seems to be clear in this paradigm of viewing the organisation as a machine is that the approach was based on:

- The "one right way".
- The premise that markets are stable and that order, rational choice and intentional capability are the only way to govern the practice of decision-making.

## How this has impacted our view of training

Figure 1.1 below (adapted from Bersin)[3] demonstrates how this paradigm has shaped our thinking in learning and development over the past years:

# Learning in a Disruptive Age

|  | Training | E-learning & Blended | Talent Management | Continuous Learning |
|---|---|---|---|---|
| **Philosophy** | Facilitator/ instructor King | Instructional design Kirkpatrick | Blended learning Social learning | 70/20/10 Taxonomies |
| **Approach** | Classroom-based instructor led | Course catalogue Online University SAQA/SETA's | Learning path Career track | Self-authored, video, mobile, YouTube |
| **Participants** | Selected few | Self-study Online learning | Career focused Lots of topics | Just in time embedded learning |
| **Technology Systems** |  | LMS as E-learning platform | LMS as talent platform | LMS as experience platform |
|  | 1970-1980 | 1998-2002 | 2005 | 2010 |

*Figure 1.1: A traditional paradigm for learning and development*

### *Training (1970 – 1980)*

Because we viewed organisations as well-oiled machines we also saw the development of people as something to improve the efficiency of the cogs in the wheel. We predominately focused on classroom-based training with the trainer being the master. People are cogs in the machine – a cog has only one job and is optimised to do that job. However, modern organisations require people to be agile and multi-functional. They need to adapt and improvise; they need to change and incorporate new and better ways of working. For example, in the movie *The Matrix*, the individual can be 'upgraded' with new skills and knowledge by simply uploading the data directly to their brain – just as one would do to a machine. Obviously this is not how people work (although how cool would that be?)

### *E-learning and blended (1998 – 2002)*

Remember Netscape? The first commercial Web browser (Netscape Navigator) was released in 1994 and in the late 1990s we realised that we as trainers could develop training through the application of technology. According to Bersin[4] the philosophy was one of an "online university" or "online course catalogue." Courses with many chapters were carefully produced by instructional designers and were accessed via an LMS (Learning or Learner Management System). There were challenges like the cost to produce the content, bandwidth issues and people's ability to access material.

This also gave rise to the concept of blended learning which unfortunately means people interpret this as add technology, stir and you have a blended approach. The MIT definition of blended learning is a lot more useful as it is defined as *"different learning or instructional methods (lecture, discussion, guided practice, reading, games, case study, simulation), different delivery methods (live classroom or computer mediated), different scheduling (synchronous or asynchronous) and different levels of guidance (individual, instructor or expert led, or group/social learning)."*[5]

In a South African context this was also the time when the Skills Development Legislation was introduced as a way of addressing the skills challenges in the country. The legislative framework was built on the principle of course catalogues, or a university.

As can be seen, the figure also refers to Kirkpatrick – a model that was first published in 1959, was updated in 1975, and again updated in 1993. In essence, this model is about evaluating the effectiveness of a training programme on four successive levels. But more about that in Chapter 5.

### Talent management (2005)

I remember that in roughly 2005 I was first introduced to the concepts of a "new way of work" or the "the future world of work". The evidence was clear that in the modern workplace the mantra was "double the work, at half the cost, at half the time, with half of the resources". We started to see organisations as systems and not machines – a network of interdependent elements that work together to accomplish the aim or its intent. Again, this also impacted on how we viewed talent management and talent development.

Also around this timeframe, LMS vendors began to find it harder to sell their stand-alone products – thus emerged talent management systems including modules on performance management, competency management, career and succession management. This was the era of the emergence of social learning (people learn from one another) and a bigger emphasis on blended learning, both as a response to an understanding that older models in the training arena were not addressing workplace challenges and that adults actually learn differently to children. Bersin[6] also indicated that in 2005, 2006 and 2007 the technologies of YouTube, Twitter and iPhone were born. These radically impacted on the way people chose to interact with content and allowed for some remarkable new learning experiences with solutions like Khan's Academy and Lynda.com.

### Continuous learning (2010)

Who can forget Corporate Leadership Council's 70/20/10 model and Bloom's Taxonomy? Around 2010 we recognised that more and more people learn regardless of whether they are in a classroom. Learning also arises naturally out of the demands and challenges of work.

What we also started to realise is that people are individuals with individualised needs and technology enabled us to deliver on these changing demands. What started to emerge and is a reality today, were paradigm shifts of physical to digital, part-brain to whole brain and compliance to play.

> **70/20/10**
> A learning philosophy that indicates effective learning should happen 70 percent of the time on-the-job learning, supported by 20 percent coaching and mentoring, and 10 percent classroom training.
>
> **Bloom's Taxonomy**
> Hierarchical model used to classify learning objectives into levels of complexity and specificity.

What we also started to realise is that people are individuals with individualised needs (different complexity levels) and technology enabled us to deliver on these changing demands. What started to emerge and is a reality today were paradigm shifts of physical to digital, part-brain to whole brain and compliance to play.

We started to explore ways and means that would accelerate learning as we experienced a world moving so much faster. Learners are now better informed and don't only want to learn but also need to be entertained. This gave rise to concepts like "edutainment" and "gamification" – Bunchball, for example, introduced the first 'modern' gamification platform in this timeframe.[7]

The obvious question is where to from here. From our perspective the modern workplace is in a state of flux and is being disrupted by some of the following forces:

- Constant introduction of disruptive technology: Replacing businesses, processes and even people.

- Accelerating digitisation and democratisation of information: Too much, overwhelmed by information, uncertainty, recipes not working.

- Quickly evolving environment: Double the work, at half the time, at half the cost, with half the resources.

> *The trends described above are dramatically changing how organisations and employees work. They demand that the modern organisation is able to respond faster and this has given rise to a number of new models – one of these being the agile organisation.*

In the next section we will first unpack the paradigm for the modern organisation and then consider the impact on learning and development for organisations.

## Entering from the side stage: the agile organisation

The concept of the agile organisation is not new. It was already introduced by Goldman, Nagel & Preiss in 1994 as a response to the need for organisations to be more adaptive to changing market conditions and to be able to respond faster.[8]

### Case in Point

*"It isn't a question of whether elephants can prevail over ants. It's a question of whether a particular elephant can dance. If it can, the ants must leave the dance floor."*
— Louis V. Gerstner Jr., *Who Says Elephants Can't Dance?*

The book mentioned above is an account of IBM's historic turnaround as told by Louis V. Gerstner, Jr., the chairman and CEO of IBM (1993 – 2002). Louis Gerstner led IBM from the brink of bankruptcy and mainframe obscurity back into the forefront of the technology business. Here he referred to a big organisation as an elephant – probably a metaphor still relevant today. And maybe even relevant to people in today's day and age who feel constrained by organisational bureaucracy and the difficulty of responding fast enough.

From our perspective agility means "teaching an elephant how to dance". For us agile is about the "being" of agile and the "doing" of agile. The difference is much more than semantics. According to Hanoulle[9] it is the distinction between "why" you are doing agile rather than "how". Agile, according to the author is, for example, more about how you approach problem solving and less about the tools used to support that approach. Agile is really a mind-set followed by the doing of agile.

*Agile organisations master – they are both stable and dynamic at the same time*

## The being of agile

Being agile is about making a conscious effort to steer away from the trusted and known and to embrace the unknown. Embracing the unknown, however, is not a case of jumping to adopt a new management fad without the slightest idea as to whether it will actually improve the business or solve the problem. It seems to us that our rapidly changing business context requires of people to be constantly curious, to be willing to let go of familiar approaches and to be able to live with the uncertainty.

## The doing of agile

It takes far more than willingness, open-mindedness and flexibility to actual apply agility (even though it starts with how we think about it). The doing of agile is about the whole organisation and its ability to be nimble in terms of direction, focus, speed, quality, and sustainability. How prepared are we to be agile when there are not 7 sign-off points in a process, or is the risk just too big for us?

The five trademarks of agile organisations à la McKinsey

For us the modern organisation is one:

- That has a sense of purpose and meaning, a keen awareness of its own identity and purpose.
- Of high involvement in the workplace with a focus on empowering people, where self-management forms the core of control and teamwork, where people are comfortably living with uncertainty.
- That values innovation, where continuous learning forms part of the values and principles of the organisation.
- That has a resilient and adaptable organisational culture.
- With a sense of urgency, coupled with a conservative approach towards finance.
- Has a keen awareness of and sensitivity towards the external environment.

In the next section we will unpack the present learning and development paradigm which is more suited to the modern place of work.

## Learning and Development: The Present

Figure 1.2 below (adapted from Bersin)[10] demonstrates the current paradigm for learning. You will also note that we are now using the words "learning" and "development" – and not "training" anymore.

Chapter 1: The past, the present and the future

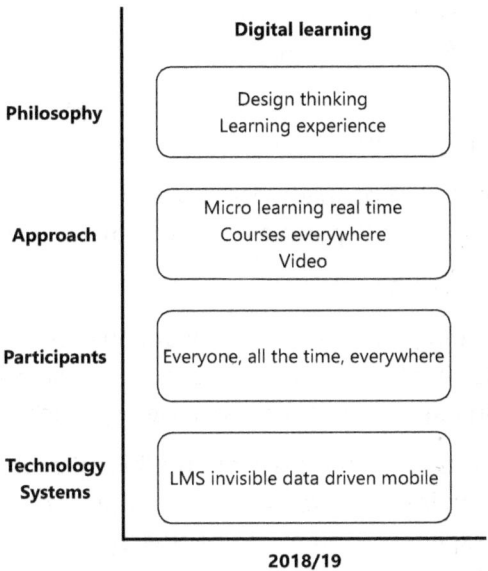

Figure 1.2: The current paradigm

The modern paradigm is one of being able to respond faster and to anticipate needs before they materialise. It is one of creating a "modern learning experience". From our perspective the following are the realities the Learning and Development practitioner will need to overcome:

- Managing the paradox of complying with legislative requirements while creating a modern learning experience.
- Creating fit-for-purpose learning solutions, solving actual business problems. The days of the traditional learning needs analysis are gone. The focus should be on "future efficiency, not past deficiency".
- Getting geared up for individualised learning, not only generic.
- Making sense of digital learning and not getting swept up in or confused by the enormous amount of technology-related learning solutions; to stay focused.
- Embedding learning as part of the job.

- Applying real-time learning that provides guidance and performance support without your people even asking.
- Moving away from traditional classroom-based learning as the only way for people to learn.
- Losing control of people's learning; learning happens despite the Learning/Training department's involvement.
- Doing more with less.
- Understanding how we measure learning – the need to shift from reporting training metrics to using learning analytics – the one being reactive, versus a proactive approach.
- It also seems to us that the more traditional cognitive models surrounding learning aren't effective or practical in the modern learning experience. What can be leveraged, improved or adapted to effectively allow people to learn? The emphasis is on social learning, spaced repetition, application of knowledge, exploration, personalised journeys, reflection, etc.
- Making optimal use of emerging technologies and infrastructures – weighing up cost versus business benefit.

## The Future: The Emerging Paradigm

The digital revolution that we see in our workplaces is fundamentally changing the way we think about people development. The reality is that people learn everywhere – in both formal and informal environments – in the lifts, during smoke and coffee breaks, in team meetings, while being coached, while reading, while "googling" the internet, in the classroom and in multiple other circumstances. So, learning cannot be controlled – it will happen beyond the reach of the learning department.

Chapter 1: The past, the present and the future

  There's a lot going on in corporate learning. This video by Josh Bersin (2019) will give you a few things to think about.[11]

For us the emerging paradigm in learning and development is actually not new. It's not a new concept that adults learn at the point of need and that learning needs to happen as part of fulfilling their job requirements. Twenty years ago we referred to it as the buddy-system where your buddy showed you what you needed to do. However, the problem with the buddy-system is twofold:

1. The buddy also teaches the learner bad habits.

2. In a modern workplace the buddy is highly likely to also not know the answer. In the future paradigm what is clear to us is that technology enables us to be more exact about the learning needs of each individual, allowing it to be integrated with current work requirements, and presented at the point of need.

For us this emerging paradigm is one of life-long learning, but how do we make sure people actually learn what they need to learn? How do we enable learning solutions for our people that are more cost-effective to design, quicker to deploy and easier to change? And, at least for now, the only way that we can see to accomplish this is to utilise the advantage of technology.

**A Moment to Reflect**

Where are the current learning paradigms in your organisation? What would you like to change/do differently?

## Summary

In this chapter we explored the past, the present and the future of learning and development. This changing way of 'doing business' is also impacting employees – they need to either gain new and different levels of competence or apply their current expertise differently. One way of doing this in a way that is faster, more cost-effective and scalable, is to use technology.

The purpose of this book is to use digital learning solutions to solve business problems. Therefore, in our next chapter we will:

1. Provide a framework for the Learning and Development practitioner in terms of the often confusing terminology in digital learning.

2. Make sense of how the disruptions mentioned within this chapter impact on how adults learn in the workplace.

# Chapter 2
## Making sense of the disruption

> *"Influential people are never satisfied with the status quo. They're the ones who constantly ask, 'What if?' and 'Why not?' They're not afraid to challenge conventional wisdom and they don't disrupt things for the sake of being disruptive; they do it to make things better."* – Travis Bradberry

## Introduction

"Disruption" seems to be the new buzzword but, as with any topic that becomes popularised, the true meaning of the concept often gets lost. The term "disruption" or more specifically, "disruptive innovation", is often accredited to Clayton Christensen and Joseph Bower in 1995.[12] They defined disruptive innovation "as a process where an inexpensive new product is launched and gradually overtakes the existing market leaders". In our modern business world, it seems to us that disruption is used synonymously with both innovation and transformation. William Pollard says, *"Learning and innovation go hand in hand. The arrogance of success is to think that what you did yesterday will be sufficient for tomorrow."* It is clear to us that there is an emerging paradigm for learning and development and we haven't found our way yet.

To create some sense in this emerging paradigm of learning that is infused with technology and geared for a different world of work, this chapter will consist of two sections:

A: Making sense of the terms used in learning technology – the purpose being creating a framework for the Learning and Development practitioner in terms of the often confusing terminology in this area.

B: Making sense of how these disruptions impact on how adults are learning in the workplace.

## Part A

In the next section we will utilise a Periodic Table of the digital learning landscape to make sense of digital learning and to unpack the key components of this landscape.

## The Periodic Table of the Digital Learning Landscape

The Periodic Table is our attempt to make sense of digital learning. From our perspective, digital learning can be described as any type of learning that is supplemented with technology or with instructional practice that makes effective use of technology. Sometimes it is confused with online learning or e-learning. From our viewpoint digital learning encompasses the aforementioned concepts and includes aspects like augmented reality, gamification and virtual reality.

In this section we will unpack these components. Please note that the authors will provide examples of vendors and tools available in the market at the point of writing, but this should not be seen as a recommendation or in any way interpreted as a reflection of the quality of the tools or the systems.

Chapter 2: Making sense of the disruption

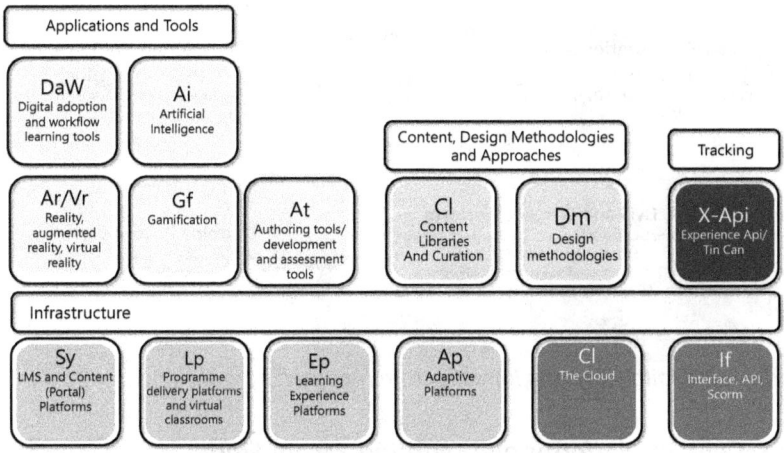

Figure 2.1: Periodic table of digital learning ©

What makes the digital landscape even more confusing is that vendor products often fall into more than one category. Learning experience platforms, for example, also tend to include an application or tool to design content seamlessly integrated within the platform.

## Infrastructure

Infrastructure refers to solutions that form the base of digital learning. In essence infrastructure connects the learner or participant with the learning content or learning experience. Often, these components also allow for tracking or some other form of analytics. Using the appropriate "infrastructure component" to best support learning is paramount – the decision on what to use should emerge from the organisational and learning strategy (more about that in the following chapter.)

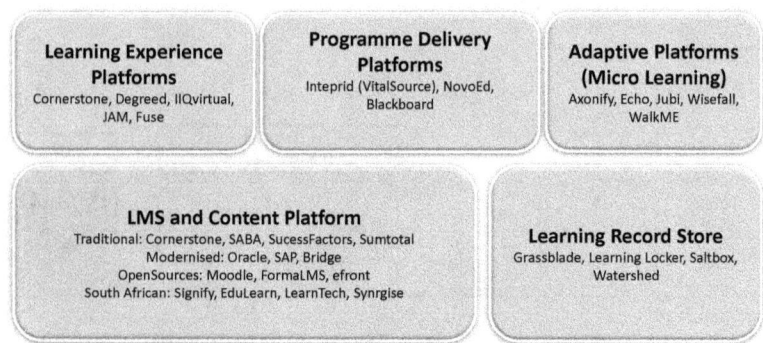

Figure 2.2: Digital Learning Infrastructure (Adapted from Josh Bersin)[13]

## LMS, Content Platforms and Learning Record Store

Learning management systems (LMS) have been a part of the digital landscape for more than 13 years. What we are experiencing currently is that the LMS industry is at a tipping point in its evolution:

- On the one hand there is pressure to provide a better learning experience. These systems were originally designed to monitor and distribute online courses tracked by a database that stores course files, learner records, assessment results and curricula.

- We are also seeing a maturity in expectations related to driving value from enterprise learning and performance support. There is a need to correlate investment in people with business metrics that actually matter.

We don't think the LMS is going away. What we do think is that it will be repositioned and enhanced by other learning technologies. What is likely to happen is that the systems that are not able to adapt will become obsolete.

Chapter 2: Making sense of the disruption

## Case in Point

### From a Company in the Financial Services Industry

An organisation's learning management system (LMS) plays an important role in the design of the learning experience, as well as deciding on the learning artefacts that will be developed. For example, if the LMS does not have a social learning functionality, then social learning components such as blogs can't be incorporated in the learning design.

As learning management systems don't always address the need for easy access to content, L&D practitioners are starting to use sharepoint sites as a portal or gateway to content. The sharepoint site is, for example, designed in such a way that a learner can access the content by selecting their role or a specific topic. This selection will then direct them to the information they need. Although the content is still housed in a central repository (as it just makes maintenance and version control so much easier) the sharepoint site guides a learner in a simple way to access information.

The implementation of learning platforms such as LinkedIn learning, Degreed, Udemy, Docebo and many more has been embraced by L&D practitioners. These platforms provide opportunities for learners to discover learning content, build skills and, in some instances, certify their expertise. As licensed learners, various topics can be searched, which unlocks a world of content. There are various ways in which learning platforms can assist the L&D function to deliver value to the business. One of the ways is through curated learning paths.

L&D practitioners working with Business and Subject Matter Experts create a learning path for a specific role. After some research, the content on the learning platform is linked to the outcome of the created learning path. The learning path is then curated on the learning platform and "pushed" to the identified recipients. Through this curation, employees in a specific role are introduced to the same content and concepts; however, this doesn't prevent learners from exploring some topics in more detail and up-skilling themselves.

Where learning platforms were introduced in organisations, it was a positive experience for the learners. They enjoyed the fact that they could look at a short video that explained, for example, a concept and that they then, when it suited them, could explore further. Although a lot of the employees didn't necessarily finish a full course that was curated for them, they did access the information they needed to build their competence.

Although learning platforms are primarily tools used by employees to up-skill themselves, they can also be used by managers in their teams. For example, a manager can identify a challenge he/she is dealing with and search for some information on the learning platform. The information selected can then be made available to all team members before a team session, as during the session the knowledge gained from the learning artefacts will be applied in discussion.

It is important to note that when learning platforms are introduced into an organisation the contextualisation must be done correctly. It is important for employees to know the reason why an organisation is implementing it and how this initiative will assist them in the execution of their jobs (e.g. to help them up-skill). If proper positioning is not done, the initial take-up will be great but over time statistical reports will indicate lack of interest and motivation.

## Chapter 2: Making sense of the disruption

*Programme Delivery Platforms*

**Lp**
Programme delivery platforms and virtual classrooms

Vendors in the programme delivery platform space provide a complete learning experience with differentiating content while giving access to full bodies of knowledge. The content often contains curated material and can include access to MOOCS. The more advanced platforms also provide a personalised learning path supported by some form analytics. When we speak of 'bodies of knowledge' we mean the complete set of concepts, terms and activities that make up a professional or vocational domain as outlined by the professional or vocational association.

*"A massive open online course (MOOC) is an online course aimed at unlimited participation and open access via the web."*

Examples of this include:

- e-MOOC
- Miriada
- OpenupEd
- Edevate
- Canvas Networks
- Virtual classrooms like traditional classrooms is an on-line learning environment where learners can engage with learning resources while working in groups and/or interact with a facilitator that guides the process and content. Some LMS systems do have a build-in classroom facility available. Other organisation utilise Zoom or Skype for such sessions.

21

Virtual classrooms: current and emerging trends

### Learning Experience Platforms

Josh Bersin coined the phrase "Learning Experience Platforms" a couple of years ago. In essence these platforms emerged as a response to the challenges experienced with the traditional LMS. Not only do people no longer search course catalogues for "courses" the way they used to, but we also need a way to develop people at point of need and integrated with work requirements (as indicated in the previous chapter). Bersin[14] lists the capabilities of experience platforms as follows:

- Content is presented in a "Netflix-like" interface, with recommendations, panels, mobile interfaces, etc.
- Any form of electronic content can be accommodated, e.g. articles, podcasts, blogs, micro-learning.
- They are social, in nature.
- There is evidence of learning paths so that content is assimilated in such a way as to achieve a logical learning outcome.
- They include forms of assessment and often badging (part of gamification) or certification.
- Individuals can publish their own content.

## Adaptive Platforms

Adaptive platforms are systems that modify the presentation of learning content in response to learner performance. What the vendors of these platforms promise is the evaluation of competence through an initial core-set of questions, virtual simulations and assigned tasks. Based on the results, the platform assesses the gap between the user knowledge and the knowledge required to meet competency requirements.

The "magic" of adaptive platforms lies in the algorithm which allows the content to be organised and delivered in ways that best suit the learner. What the algorithm does is to identify the most effective learning modality (visual, auditory, kinesthetic and tactile) and then recommends the next best steps the learner should take to master the content.

Examples include:

- ALEKS
- SmartUp (also considered a micro-learning platform)
- Smart Sparrow

## Interfaces and the Cloud

In this section we will only unpack the most commonly used terms (there are more but it is likely you will come across these most often):

- API stands for Application Programming Interface. It is a generic software term for the connection between different technical systems. Two software systems can share defined data with each other using APIs.
- As a standard, Shareable Content Object Reference Model (SCORM) is primarily used to bridge the gap between eLearning authoring tools and LMS systems. SCORM is the de facto specification for packaging learning content and is a standard

format which allows the package to work in different LMSs. Although it is extensively used in LMSs, it is reaching its sell-by date and is being replaced by APIs.

■ The "Cloud" is just a shorthand term for "cloud computing", which itself just refers to the idea of using someone else's computers (usually, but not always, operated by a business) on the Internet for things we previously used our own for, like storing data and running programmes.

## Applications and Tools

These are all software applications and tools to design content and learning experiences. As previously indicated, some of the applications and tools are already integrated into digital platforms; others need different devices to be delivered to the learner or participant.

*Digital adoption and workflow learning tools*

**DaW**
Digital adoption and workflow learning tools

When confronted with a clogged drain it is unlikely that you will sign up for a full course on plumbing. Most people "google the answer", or would watch a video on YouTube. Similarly, employees seek quick resolution to the problems or questions they encounter at work and a course is not necessarily the answer. Digital adoption and workflow tools (also known as Electronic Performance Support Systems – EPSS), help employees to work more efficiently. Users are supported in their work tasks and they learn within the workflow with guidance from the tool. Examples of these include WalkMe (that markets itself as a digital adoption platform) and WhatFix.

Case Study: BMC Software, Inc.
An American technology company that produces software and services that assist businesses in moving to digital operations.

Chapter 2: Making sense of the disruption

## Artificial Intelligence

Artificial intelligence[15] (AI) is "the simulation of human intelligence processes by machines. These processes include learning (the acquisition of information and rules for using the information), reasoning (using rules to reach approximate or definite conclusions) and self-correction".

**Ai** — Artificial Intelligence

AI will make it possible to assess and recommend tailored learning solutions quickly. Though not yet a reality, the ultimate goal in this field seems to be the "creation of virtual human-like characters" who can think, act, react and interact in a natural way, responding to and using both verbal and nonverbal communication. This could be very useful when a person needs to learn how to interact with people in a specific environment in a non-linear way. The AI entity is able to adapt to the situation based on different inputs, creating a more realistic learning environment. The AI is also able to 'learn' and add new branches and responses based on past experience.

Article: Artificial Intelligence in Corporate Training: Myths and Predictions.

## Reality, augmented and virtual reality

**Ar/Vr** — Reality, augmented reality, virtual reality

Virtual reality is an immersive interactive computer-generated experience taking place within a simulated environment. It incorporates mainly auditory and visual feedback, but may also allow other types of sensory feedback from gloves and other wearable inputs. This immersive environment can be similar to the real world or it can be fantastical. Virtual reality can be a powerful tool in situations where the real world is too dangerous for learning to take place (e.g. fire-fighting or combat training).

Augmented reality is technology that overlays information and virtual objects on real-world scenes in real time. It uses the existing environment and adds information to it to make a new artificial and augmented environment. Augmented reality is particularly effective where the subject material is too expensive or cumbersome to be used in a learning environment (e.g. aircraft engines or complicated mechanical tools).

Case Study: 9 Powerful Real-World Applications of Augmented Reality (AR) Today

### Gamification

Though the term "gamification" was coined in 2002 by Nick Pelling,[16] a British-born computer programmer and inventor, it did not gain popularity until 2010. The concept is usually defined as *"the use of game thinking and game mechanics in non-game contexts to engage users in solving problems and increase users' self-contributions"*. From a leadership development perspective two examples in particular have emerged that show how gamification platforms are being leveraged to develop future leaders. Both NTT DATA (a systems integration company) and the well-known consulting company Deloitte, use gamification successfully. Both organisations claim that what makes this so successful is the ability to use game mechanics to drive greater levels of engagement and employee motivation.

**Gf**
Gamification

> It is important to note that gamification should not be just about fun. It should be consistent with an organisation's analytics-driven approach to workforce management and aligned to their business goals.

## Authoring tools/development and assessment tools

In the context of learning and development, an authoring tool refers to software used to create digital learning content. This is often referred to as e-learning (electronic learning) or m-learning (mobile learning). The purpose of an authoring tool is to make developing content more effective and efficient and remove the need for complex coding skills. An example could be adding hotspots (allowing for learners to interact with the content) to an image that would take hours to manually code. Most authoring tools allow you to do this in a few clicks.

Some of the features and functionality that authoring/development tools include are as follows:

- eLearning authoring tools usually offer the ability to develop slide-based e-learning with interactive elements. Generally, these tools will allow output of content to multiple formats like HTML5, SCORM or Tin Can. Some of these applications – called responsive design authoring tools – also allow content to be distributed via multiple platforms, e.g. mobile devices. Examples include Articulate Storyline, Captivate, Lectora and iSpring as well as a number of free tools.
- Video Capture and Editing tools allow the design and editing of software simulations and other assets into professional-looking videos. Some even allow for internal assessments and knowledge checks. Often, videos are embedded in a course developed in an eLearning authoring tool.
- Some learning platforms, as previously mentioned, also allow the ability to develop a range of content and assessments.

E-book: Decoding Mobile Learning - A Handy Guide

**Awesome apps for learning practitioners**

Daniel Jones[1] was so kind as to put together the following list of applications for learning practitioners that you may find useful:

| Presentations | Social Images | Videos | Animations | Infographics |
|---|---|---|---|---|
| Canva<br>Haiku Deck<br>PopBoardz<br>Visme | Assembly<br>Spark Post<br>Stencil<br>Whom<br>Wordle | iMovie<br>Magisto<br>Premiere Clip<br>Spark Video | Moovly<br>GoAnimate<br>MySimpleShow<br>PowToon | Infogram<br>LucidChart<br>Piktochart<br>Venngage |
| **Quizzes/Polls** | **Stories** | **AR** | **Photo Editing** | **Other** |
| Kahoot<br>Mentimeter<br>Poll Everywhere | Inklewriter<br>Twine | HP Reveal<br>ThingLink | Microsoft Pix<br>Snapseed | Storyboard That<br>Office Lens<br>Post It Plus |

## Content, Design Methodologies and Approaches

In this part of our periodic table we will briefly touch on content and design methodologies. When one considers learning content there tend to be three choices:

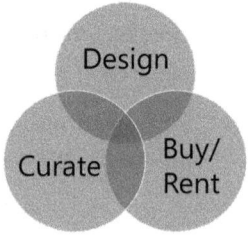

---

1   linkedin.com/in/dwjones/

*Content curation*

It is actually unbelievable how much content is available on the web today and much of it free. It makes one consider the rationale of developing content oneself. Content curation is an approach that involves the discovering, gathering and presenting of existing digital content based on specific subject matter/learning needs. Instead of designing in-house content, the curator reviews what is available and what is appropriate to the organisation's environment. Examples here include the popular TED-Talks and YouTube videos.

*Buy/Rent*

Buy or rent is an approach where content is purchased from a third-party supplier. Examples (and there are literally hundreds) include:

- Coursera that partners with universities like Stanford, Johns Hopkins, Duke and more, to offer college or university courses online.
- LinkedIn Learning which is geared towards courses for professional skills. It offers over 1 000 options including topics like **Time Management Fundamentals**, **Customer Service Foundations**, and **Discovering Your Strengths**.
- edX which is similar to Coursera. It is a non-profit organisation that offers thousands of courses to anyone and includes subjects like Business and Management, Chemistry, and Philanthropy, as well as degree programmes.
- The Great Courses (TGC) which is slightly different from the above services. Instead of partnering with colleges and offering free courses, TGC offers more practical courses at individual costs. You'll find professional courses like The Entrepreneur's Toolkit and The Art of Negotiating the Best Deal, but it also offers courses like Fundamentals of Photography, How to Draw, and Secrets of Mental Math.

## Design

The final option here is to design programmes specific to your purpose. We will in the next chapter talk a bit more about design principles and the choices here. But what is true is that digital learning design is in its essence an art and a science. You need to be able to apply the principles of proper learning design as well as focus on the learning experience and engage the learner.

How much does it cost?

This link will provide you with information on what it could cost to design e-learning/online course material.

This link will provide you with information on what a virtual reality training simulator could cost.

### A Moment to Reflect

Having reviewed the Periodic Table of the Digital Learning Landscape – what are your current insights? Do you have concerns? Questions that need to be answered?

Now that we have unpacked the digital learning landscape with all the different elements, it is important to also consider how people think about digital learning and the misconceptions that often exist. Perhaps some of these may clarify some of the concerns you have raised above.

Chapter 2: Making sense of the disruption

## Digital Myths

In the last part of Section A of this book we would like to also unpack and clarify a few misconceptions or myths with regard to the digital learning landscape. Most of these are based on our own experiences and interactions with a number of companies over the past years.

**Myth #1:** *Learner outcomes are not as good with digital learning and it is not suitable for teaching certain skills*

Our opinion here is that the problem does not lie with the concept of digital learning, but more how the learning content is designed. You cannot follow the same design approach for digital learning as you do for a classroom-based approach. Learning outcomes can be just as good (if not better) if one applies a proper design methodology and approach. We do agree that learning focused on social skills will not have a 100% similar outcome. (As one person mentioned to us – the AHA moment is just not the same. That magic that is created in the classroom when the self-insight happens – is just not the same.) This, however, can be easily addressed through a blended learning approach. Our opinion is that what needs to change is how we think about digital learning design and application.

Case in Point

VirtualSpeech is an example of an app that lets you practise social skills in front of a realistic virtual audience.

31

### Myth #2: There is no real cost saving by adopting digital learning

The design of digital content (and the computing devices like smartphone and VR readers) is usually expensive and has created a perception that the adoption of digital learning doesn't really result in cost saving. Here one needs to consider to overall value of digital learning within the organisation. Karla Gutierrez[17] unpacks the value of digital learning as follows:

- Digital learning has faster delivery cycle times than traditional, classroom-based instruction. It is not limited by the number of available trainers and classrooms.

- Digital learning requires from 40% to 60% less employee time than the same material delivered in a traditional classroom setting. It immediately eliminates direct delivery costs including transportation, accommodation, printing time and distribution. Consequently, it improves employee productivity since it's considerably quicker than the classroom-based alternative.

- Digital learning is easier, cheaper and quicker to update and is very suitable to scale quickly.

The question one sometimes needs to ask is: The design of digital learning is expensive in comparison to what – the loss of a life, the loss of a customer?

### Myth #3: Digital learning is not effective when used with disadvantaged populations

Digital learning can be successfully implemented with a broad range of beneficiaries across ages, geographical regions, backgrounds and socioeconomic conditions. However, some groups would be more successful if they received preparatory initiatives prior to partaking in digital learning. We refer to this as learning onboarding and digital adoption. Chapter 4 will provide you with more information on how to deal with this challenge.

We have also seen that this has led to some unintended positive consequences for a company in the Retail space. Digital learning actually enhanced performance and reduced mistakes, shrinkage and rework. People started to upskill cross-functionally (without anyone managing and controlling the process) resulting in a true culture of learning and performance.

### Myth #4: It is too difficult for beneficiaries to use digital learning due lack of computing devices and network access

This is probably one of the most difficult barriers. However, it has been proven possible to overcome and work around information and communication hurdles in nearly every environment. It requires careful planning, taking into consideration what is currently available that can be leveraged. It asks for the courage to open our minds and to think differently.

### Myth #5: Digital learning puts the facilitator's job at risk

A recent study found that digital learning typically requires from 40% to 60% less instructor or facilitator time than the same material delivered in a traditional classroom setting.[18] This can be seen as either a threat or an opportunity for facilitators. The freeing up of time allows the facilitators to re-skill themselves and to transition to a new andragogy – how adults learn in a digital space. It also allows facilitators to undertake more one-to-one coaching, or engage with individuals on a personal basis in areas of specific need.

### Myth #6: Digital learning is not social

This was one of the biggest mistakes made in our industry (and admittedly one we made ourselves) – we forgot that humans are social in nature and that they learn using social interaction. Successfully deploying digital learning doesn't remove the social component of learning. Social Cognitive Theory is a formal theory of learning that asserts that people learn from observing others in their social environments. Technology increases our abilities to provide models for students/learners to observe and to practise skills. It is also important to remember that digital learning does not replace the social interaction needs of people.

## Summary

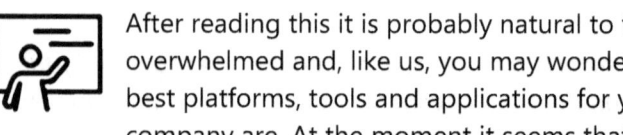

After reading this it is probably natural to feel totally overwhelmed and, like us, you may wonder what the best platforms, tools and applications for your company are. At the moment it seems that multiple technologies are the answer, but you may wish for that one tool that can provide an integrated experience. What is even more important is that the integrated "tool" or "platform" also needs to cater for other aspects of talent management like on-boarding and performance support. This one integrated "tool" or "platform" is probably the way of the future as we are already seeing these needs and solutions in business-related platforms and applications.

In the next chapter we will unpack a framework for you to make sense of your digital strategy and hopefully this will assist to make some sense of a solution for your organisation. What this chapter has also highlighted is the need for a collaborative partnership between the Learning and Development and IT Departments. In Chapter 4 we will provide you with some more tips on how to optimise the relationship so that the experts can decode the IT speak into English.

In the next section of this book we will introduce you to the modern learner.

## Part B

## Meet the modern learner

If you ask business people "how people learn," their most common answer is "on the job" and this seems to be true – sales people learn by making sales calls, engineers learn by doing design, train drivers learn by driving trains. The key to success then is not to provide a lot of formal training, but rather to create an environment that supports rapid on-the-job learning. However, what has changed fundamentally is the time people have available to learn. This and the way consumerism has changed has had a serious impact on the expectations of the modern learner. Just as the modern consumer wants to be in control, wants to be able to shop 24/7, share their experiences and wants to treated as individuals, the modern learner shares similar expectations:

| Expectations: The Past | Expectations: The Present and Emerging Future |
| --- | --- |
| <ul><li>Learning methods are limited and we understand that. I in any case prefer to "go to training" and get away from work.</li><li>Not a lot changes, the content I need to do my job stays the same. I just need refresher training from time to time.</li><li>The facilitator or my manager knows everything. All I need I will get from them.</li><li>I didn't like it when I needed to learn things that weren't immediately relevant to my job, but it was ok.</li></ul> | <ul><li>I want to choose from a variety of learning methods as and when it suits me.</li><li>Everything around me is changing. I need updated learning content helping me to upskill myself faster.</li><li>No one knows everything. I also have learnings to contribute. Allow me space to share.</li><li>I'm busy and don't have time to waste. Don't waste my time by teaching me things I can't apply immediately.</li></ul> |

> **A Moment to Reflect**
>
> What are some of the expectations in your organisation?

As part of your designing your digital learning strategy, you need to consider the modern learner – who they are, what they expect and how your digital learning strategy will add value to them. In this section we will highlight for you some of the key features of the modern learner as outlined by Bersin[19] as well as some of our own observations and experiences:

## Key features of the modern learner

### Untethered and distributed

Currently, a lot of employees find themselves working from several locations and structuring their work in non-traditional ways to accommodate their lifestyles and work requirements. In the South African context 'workplace' also doesn't necessarily mean a localised office. Companies and training departments are finding it difficult to reach these people and even harder to develop them efficiently.

### Overwhelmed and time-strapped

A famous saying we have is that the modern employee needs to do *"double the work, at half the time, at half the cost, with half the resources"*. This leaves very little time for learning and research is suggesting that only approximately 24 minutes a week per employee is available in their busy work lives. This very clearly implies that we need to rethink our traditional models of days and days of classroom-based learning.

Chapter 2: Making sense of the disruption

*Demanding and on-demand*

Consumerism and "available on demand" has impacted the modern learner's need to access learning at the point of need. Just as we can choose what entertainment we want to watch at what time (the Netflix approach) we also want answers when we need them. The modern learner is looking for answers outside of traditional training and development channels – "we google the answers we need". The dilemma with this is that you have no control over the appropriateness of the learning content to your organisational context and requirements.

*Collaborative*

Learners are also developing and accessing personal and professional networks to obtain information about their industries and professions. Up to 80% of workforce learning happens via on-the-job interactions with peers, team-mates and managers.

InfoGraphic

The profile of the modern learner

*The challenge of recalling information*

> *"To understand something, you must actively engage with it."*

Were you ever in a situation where you just can't recall what you have read or were introduced to in a classroom? It's a hazy, foggy thing which is often vague and unclear. Part of the challenge with the modern learner is that information is overwhelming and that most do not have a cognitive model to recall the information that they were exposed to. What you want is for people to be exposed to content/ information/ theory or whatever, and then we want them to engage with the practical application of it. And then we want them to repeat it so that it actually starts to embed itself into our long-term memory.

At this stage in time you may also wonder if there are differences between how different generations learn in the workplace:

## Multi-generational learning

We know that by 2020, most companies will have four or five generations working together. These individuals often have fundamentally different experiences that can lead them to communicate differently. They also differ in terms of the value they place on different things in the workplace. Much has been said and written on this topic – but the question does remain – what does it mean from a learning and development perspective? Research is available in terms of how the different generations learn, but we do wonder if it is just too generic in nature

We also think that a lot of the research emphasises the millennial in the workforce. As Generation X-ers we feel a little neglected and excluded. If we move beyond just our own personal feelings on this GenX will be approximately 25% of the workforce and will be the next generation of leadership within the organisation – making their development still extremely important.

From a multi-generation perspective, we suggest that you consider the following within your strategy:

### Personalise the experience

As far as possible rather personalise the learning experience instead of broad brush strokes of generalisation. Personalisation means that you provide the appropriate learning for an employee in a way that maximises retention and application on the job. You may want to ask:

- What learning methods did the learner become accustomed to as part of formal education? What impact will that have on the way they learn?

- What social influences affected learning and engagement in the learning process? Are they for example more geared to team or individual activities?

*Make the experience engaging*

Do consider that learning engagement is largely affected by an individual's specific motivation for learning. Some people learn for the sake of learning, but most learn at the point of need – they have a problem to solve. With the changing technological and social landscape, generations aren't necessarily engaged by the same factors. To provide effective learning solutions to a multi-generational workforce, you will need to employ a variety of engagement mechanisms that resonate with all employees.

*How adults learn*

You also need to consider how adults actually learn, especially the modern employee dealing with modern workplace challenges. You may want to consider:

- **How you present learning experiences.** With shorter timeframes available for learning, chunking may be a suitable approach. Chunking is the process of developing information on a single narrow topic and delivering it in a short, simple and memorable way. It is also known as micro-learning. We think chunking is useful across different generations as it caters for both shorter attention-spans of younger generation and memory decline of older generations.

- **How you make sure that people can actively recall learning experiences at point of need.** Active recall is the process of actually retrieving information from memory – when a question is asked, e.g. product knowledge – can a suitable answer be provided?

- **How you apply the principles of continuous learning re-inforcement.** This is the process of providing information to learners in a repetitive and consistent way that reinforces a prior learning event, such as a workshop, improving the retention of the knowledge.

> **A Moment to Reflect**
>
> How does the modern learner look in your organisation? What are the challenges and opportunities you are facing?

## The skills for the future

We don't think a section on the modern learner can be complete without referring to the emerging and future skills, we as learning practitioners need to cater for. The World-Economic Forum[20] report on the "Future of Jobs" reports that the skill sets required in both old and new occupations will change in most industries and transform how and where people work. So not only does your digital learning strategy need to cater for "how" people can learn better in a disruptive way, but also for "what" they learn and how you will make sure that you create future-fit employees.

According to the Institute for Future Research[21] many studies over the years attempted to predict job requirements for the future. However, it has been shown that such predictions are difficult and many of the past predictions have been proven wrong. Rather than focusing on future jobs, the Institute recommends that we rather look at future work skills – proficiencies and abilities required across different jobs and work settings. Their predictions for 2020 include:

Chapter 2: Making sense of the disruption

Skills required to deal with the rise of smart machines and technology
- Sense-making
- Novel and adaptive thinking
- Social intelligence

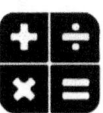

Skills required to deal with the computational world (massive increase in sensors and computational power)
- Cognitive load management
- Computational thinking
- Trans-disciplinary

Skills required to deal with the new media ecology
- New media literacy
- Cognitive load management
- Computational thinking

Skills to deal with super-structured organisations and global connectedness
- Design mind-set
- Cross cultural competency
- Virtual collaboration

## Summary

In this chapter we looked specifically at the forces that are causing the disruption in the workplace and how these call for a rethink of our own learning and development practices. We also unpacked the being and the expectations of the modern learner. Lastly, we looked at predictions in terms of future skill requirements and how that asks of the modern learning practitioner to in their digital learning strategy design not only cater for "how" people learn but also for "what" they learn.

# Chapter 3
## Designing a Digital Learning Strategy

> "Students do not learn much just sitting in classes listening to teachers, memorizing pre-packaged assignments, and spitting out answers. They must talk about what they are learning, write reflectively about it, relate it to past experiences, and apply it to their daily lives. They must make what they learn part of themselves." – Arthur W. Chickering and Stephen C. Ehrmann

## Introduction

### The Emperor's New Clothes by Hans Christian Andersen

In this story, the Emperor loves fine clothing. Two men, swindlers, arrive in the city claiming to be the best weavers imaginable. They claim that the clothing they make is the finest with beautiful, intricate patterns. The swindlers say that this clothing is also magical and would appear invisible to anyone who was stupid or incompetent.

The Emperor is excited about this amazing product, and he pays the men a huge sum to make these magnificent clothes. The swindlers then pretended to weave and sew the clothing with empty looms and needles without thread. The Emperor sends men to check on the swindlers' work.

> When each man realises he sees nothing, he does not want to admit it for fear he would be accused of being stupid and incompetent. So, each man lies to the Emperor, saying how the clothing was magnificent.
>
> The clothing is brought to the Emperor on the day of a great procession. The Emperor sees nothing, but he, too, did not want to admit to being stupid or incompetent, so he agrees that the clothing is exquisite. After being dressed in the invisible garments, the Emperor marches in the procession in front of his entire kingdom. Everyone in the kingdom sees the emperor without clothes, but for fear of being accused of being stupid or incompetent, they all sing the false praises of their Emperor's fine clothing.
>
> Finally, a child says, "But he doesn't have anything on!"[22]
>
> Source: https://study.com/academy/lesson/the-emperors-new-clothes-summary-moral.html

*The Emperor's New Clothes* reminds us that like the modern-day example of technology, the question that still remains is whether there is value in what we create through our learning experiences. We should not be mesmerised by technology simply because it is so admired. Sometimes it is just okay for the Emperor to cover the most important bits. Larry Cuban, a researcher and writer, penned the following:

> *"Since 2010, laptops, tablets, interactive whiteboards, smart phones, and a cornucopia of software have become ubiquitous. We spent billions of dollars on computers. Yet has academic achievement improved as a consequence? Has teaching and learning changed? Has use of devices in schools led to better jobs? These are the basic questions that school boards, policy makers, and administrators ask. The answers to these questions are 'no,' 'no,' and 'probably not.'"*[23]

As you have seen from our previous chapters there is an abundance of new digital learning companies, initiatives and innovations that have emerged across the education and learning industry in the last couple of years. As with any kind of innovation some of these initiatives have been successful, while others were sometimes very expensive failures. This, of course, fuelled our own scepticism around the efficacy of digital learning. We don't think the issue is with the technology; we think the challenge modern Learning and Development practitioners are facing is to make it work within organisations. Therefore, the purpose of this chapter is to help you to critically evaluate your own thinking on the what, why and how of digital learning.

In the next chapter we will share with you some lessons learnt by ourselves and our colleagues in the industry who kindly shared their experiences with us.

## A thinking framework

If there's one thing you can bet on when the word 'strategy' is mentioned it is that most of these documents or meetings hinge on two elements: a SWOT (strengths, weaknesses, opportunities, threats) analysis and some sort of vision and mission statements. Yet, we have never seen how this actually has an impact on an organisation's results, never mind that of a Learning and Development Department or unit. For purposes of this chapter in the book we will utilise the learning and development landscape as a thinking framework in order to make sure we capture all the elements of a digital strategy that will actually have an impact:

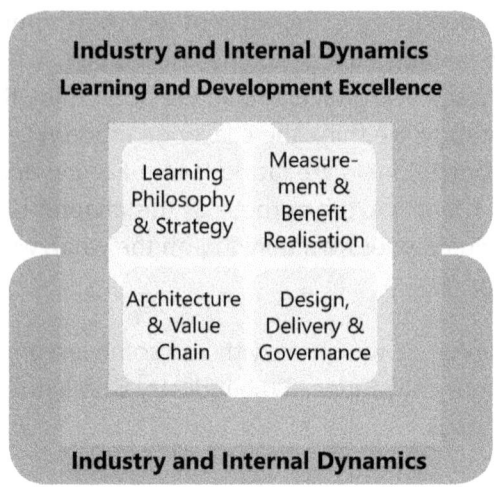

*Figure 3.1: The learning and development landscape*

These can be seen as the different building blocks of your strategy.

## Industry and internal dynamics and the regulatory environment

> *Just because something doesn't do what you planned it to do doesn't mean it's useless.* - Thomas Edison (Inventor)

As we continue to use and engage technology at varying degrees of complexity – or simplicity – in our Learning and Development environments, it is okay to be charmed by the technological trends, the sometimes hype and sometimes overwhelming innovation in this regard. But it is important to recognise that digital learning must be used appropriately, and not as the be-all and end-all solution to every performance opportunity and learning problem. One of the biggest mistakes we think Learning and Development practitioners make is to get excited about the technology, and engage with vendors without really understanding the challenges the industry is facing and their own internal dynamics. As you are probably well aware, the learning landscape in South Africa is highly regulated and hasn't always kept up with technological advances globally.

Chapter 3: Designing a Digital Learning Strategy

By unpacking these dynamics, you will hopefully answer the questions on why a digital learning strategy, and clearly build a business case on what business challenges or opportunities you are addressing. We think now is the time to challenge our institutional and regulatory practices. We need to introduce scalable and sustainable practices that better leverage that which technology can provide to deliver a faster, agile and personalised learning experience for both the individual and the organisation.

## Unpacking the environment

The following steps apply

**Step 1:** Unpack the challenges that you face in terms of both industry and regulatory environment. The template below highlights aspects for you to consider:

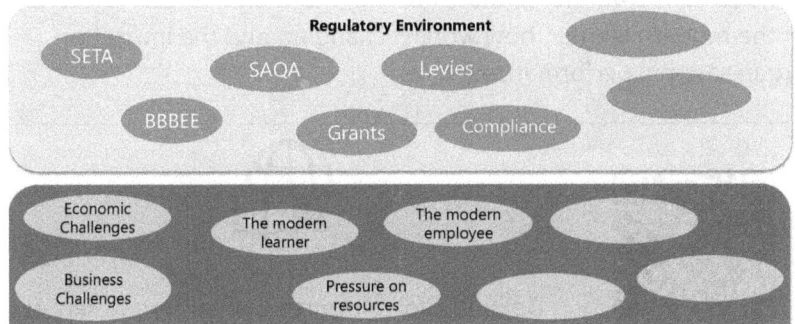

Step 2: Identify which of these can be addressed through digital learning. You may want to consider wording it as 'risks/opportunities' and how digital learning can help you address these risks/opportunities:

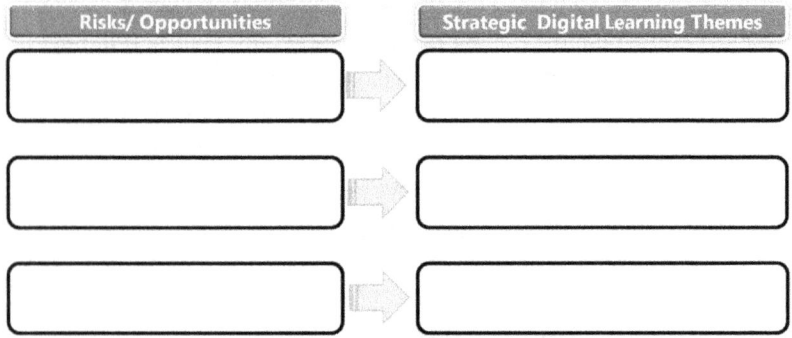

You may find it useful at this stage to also review the Deloitte Global Human Capital Trends Report. The report states that *"People now rate the 'opportunity to learn' as among their top reasons for taking a job, and business leaders know that changes in technology, longevity, work practices, and business models have created a tremendous demand for continuous, lifelong development"*.[24] It provides some insight on the alternative workforce that is talking more on the requirements of the modern learner, how work is changing and the impact on organisational performance.

Deloitte Global Human Capital Trends Report

## Learning Philosophy and Strategy

The Learning Philosophy answers the questions on how we think about learning and how it will add value. It also addresses the question of the purpose and the role of the Learning and Development Department or unit within the organisation.

Chapter 3: Designing a Digital Learning Strategy

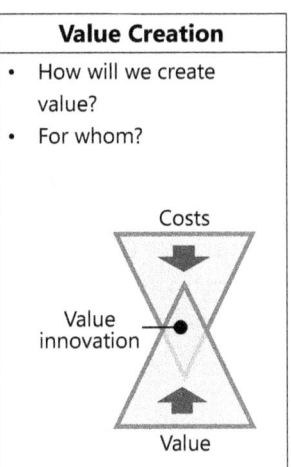

## Defining the learning philosophy

Your learning philosophy will answer the following questions:

- How will digital learning help us to solve our business problems/opportunities?
- How will we know we are successful?
- How do we think about learning and development (our approach)?
- What value will we create/for whom?
  - How much value will they attach to what we are offering?
- What is the state of our learning culture and what should it be?
- What is our role as a Learning and Development Department?

In order to guide you in answering these question we will share with you a number of ideas and templates:

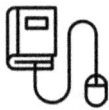

*How will digital learning help us to solve our business problems/opportunities?*

- Identify the value drivers of introducing digital learning.

49

- Consolidate these findings into a business case to project net impact for the organisation.
- Examine potential risks or barriers to success.

*How will we know we are successful?*

This question answers how you will, through your digital learning strategy, address the business challenge or opportunity. How do you actually know that the strategy has achieved what you've intended it to achieve?

Some examples here can include:

| Meeting learning needs at point of need | Addressing personal learning needs, learning more self-directed | Measuring what actually matters |
|---|---|---|
| Engaging learning culture throughout the organisation | Learning that has an impact on business performance | Learning is more accessible to all, we can scale easily |

*How do we think about learning and development?*

There are many learning philosophies and theories and they are difficult to "categorise" as they often overlap and are subject to individual interpretations and viewpoints. But this will be a key question you need to answer because it will have a fundamental impact on how you think about learning design and delivery. The analysis of your industry and organisation should guide you in what is most appropriate to your context. This kind of questioning, however, makes us think of the warning of George Box:

Chapter 3: Designing a Digital Learning Strategy

*"Remember that all models are wrong; the practical question is how wrong do they have to be to not be useful?"* Your answers here are not cast in stone, but they will help you to understand the "why" behind some of your own practices.

We are going to oversimplify now, but roughly, philosophies about learning and development (and education) can be divided into four broad categories:

| Behaviourism | Focuses on observable behaviour and "combines elements of philosophy, methodology, and psychological theory". This links closely to the competency-based approach within learning and development. |
|---|---|
| Constructivism | Concerned with the nature of knowledge, to really simplify – focuses on how humans make meaning in relation to the interaction between their experiences and their ideas. |
| Cognitivism | Focuses on mental processes and is concerned with how people receive, process and organise information. |
| Connectivism | Emphasises the role of the social and cultural context and views learning as "a process of pattern recognition". |

**Holistic approach to Technology Enhanced Learning**

The Learning Exploratorium Labs focused on research on eLearning quality and provide broad recommendations for consideration by decision makers, industry, research and teachers or training entities.

This link will take you to an infographic.

51

> *MIT blended learning definition*
>
> Structured opportunities to learn, which use more than one learning or training method, inside or outside the classroom.[25]

You are trying to answer the question on how adults in your organisational context learn and what approach will work best/or a combination of approaches. This is also where you need to think about the concept of blended learning and the mixture of your blend. No, we are not referring to classroom-based learning where you add technology and now it's blended. We will talk a bit more about this when we discuss learning architecture.

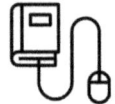

### How much value will we create/for whom?

Value and creating value is one of those organisational buzzwords, often used, often misunderstood. The dilemma with value is that people will perceive it very differently and what is regarded as value for one stakeholder doesn't necessarily hold true for all. We also think that part of the dilemma is that we as Learning and Development practitioners also have a very inward focus when we think of value. We ask how we will add value – and don't necessarily consider whether our stakeholders will view this as valuable.

In an attempt to address this, you may have come across the term "learner-centric design". Learner-centric design means the emphasis is on the learner, their needs, skills, learning motivation etc. Traditionally learning tended to focus more on the content, instead of the learning experience we intended to create. Part of your philosophy and strategy very clearly needs to define what value you will create for whom. Here you should ask questions like what learners would like to see or experience in a learning system. How will it solve the business problems they are encountering?

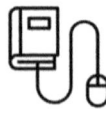

### Learning culture

We know that culture is one of the major performance differentiators in the modern organisation. Culture creates

the foundation for strategy execution, people performance and customer delight, and will either be a company's greatest asset or largest liability. To successfully implement a digital learning culture it could be beneficial to evaluate your current learning culture in terms of audience readiness, leadership support and other aspects of culture you may need to address. Brainstorm what your new learning culture will need to look like, feel like and what will need to change.

You may want to consider asking:

- What is the current attitude and orientation towards learning?
- To what extent do you have leadership support and buy-in?
- Do leaders know and understand their role in learning?
- How open are people to adopting new technology?

### Purpose and role of the Learning and Development Department

Evaluate the purpose and the role of the Learning and Development Department in a digital world. Brainstorm what your new role and purpose will need to look like, feel like and what will need to change. Also consider your team's mind-set and identify strengths and areas you will need to address. Assess current skillsets and identify role changes that will need to happen in order to take your team into a digital learning future. Make a plan for keeping your team current with the knowledge needed to excel in a digital learning future.

## Formulating the strategic objectives

The next questions to answer are:

- Given the issues, assumptions and learning philosophy, what options do we have from a digital perspective?
- Given the options, what are the key strategic priorities for Learning and Development?

Example of a Digital Learning Strategy with emphasis on the Strategic Objectives

## Architecture and Value Chain

In this section we will unpack the requirements for the learning architecture and value chain.

### Learning architecture

Learning architecture translates the learning philosophy and strategy into the physical operating model of the unit within the organisation responsible for learning and development. The architecture also ensures that development and capacity building are aligned to other processes within the sphere of Human Capital, e.g. talent management.

The operating model or architecture pertains to the 'logic' required by the unit within the organisation responsible for Learning and Development to establish, unlock and deliver ongoing value with respect to learning and development. An effective operating model must be informed by the following design principles (or design criteria):

- Purpose: Clarity on the business problem and/or requirement to address it.
- Clear ownership, responsibilities and accountabilities.
- Simplicity.
- Minimisation of duplication.

- Allows for standardisation, agility/flexibility.
- Value-add.
- Tight (i.e. centralisation) and loose (i.e. decentralisation).
- Direct line of sight between actions and results/outcomes.
- Involvement/participation.
- Cost-effectiveness.
- Responsiveness.
- Customisation/localisation.
- Integration/seamlessness.

How you choose to apply the different elements is a function of your own organisational context.

## The digital learning value chain

The term "value chain" describes a way of looking at a business or an industry as a chain of activities that transform inputs and outputs into customer value. Customer value is derived from three basic sources: activities that differentiate the product, activities that lower its cost and activities that meet the customer's need quickly.[26]

The digital learning value chain disaggregates your digital learning strategy into relevant processes and activities in order to understand the costs, the resource requirements and the existing and potential sources of value for the individual as well as for the organisation.

The diagram below is an example of such a digital learning value chain and it could assist in benchmarking your own process.

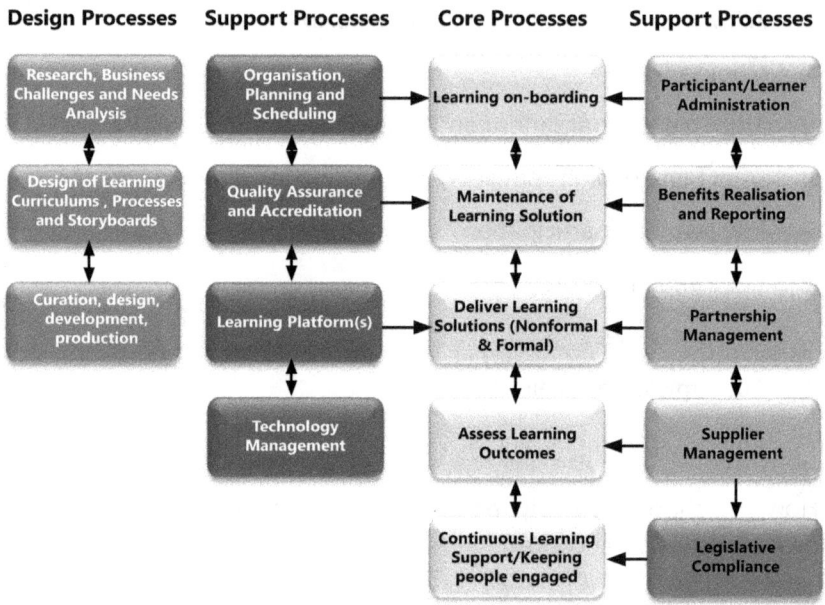

*Figure 3.1: The digital learning value chain*

### Technology Architecture

The Technology Architecture is a description of the structure and interaction of the platform(s) and other logical and physical technology components, like authoring tools, video editing tools, etc.

In order to build the Technology Architecture, you need to list the requirements that your digital tools and platforms should meet (platforms, tools, LMS, infrastructure) in order to create the sort of experience you want and the data you want to track. We also suggest that you draw your current Technology Architecture and evaluate it against your desired or new technical requirements. Map your desired Technology Architecture and devise ways to fill the gaps.

You may want to ask:

- What kind of experiences do we want to create?
- Do we need to scale – to what extent?

Chapter 3: Designing a Digital Learning Strategy

- How cost effective is this?
- Is this the right fit for the business?
- How big is the budget?
- What are the implications for computing devices (e.g. laptop, smartphone, access to data) for learners?
- How digitally literate are employees? Do we need additional support?

Some examples here can include:

| Learner-centric and easy to use | Fit for purpose | Allows for rapid and agile content development and deployment |
|---|---|---|
| Strong customer support by vendor | Provides learning in multiple languages | Can integrate with other talent management systems |

In terms of your Technology Architecture you may need to also consider:

- Will you Reuse, Build or Buy? Decisions on further development or replacement of legacy system are informed by guiding principles set out in the Learning Philosophy and Strategy and the financial implications.
- The current policies and standards to guide the selection and implementation of particular technology elements already in existence in your organisation.

- The extent to which security systems are integrated with software applications.
- The suitability of other software applications deployed within an organisation, especially some other talent or HR systems.
- People's access to computing devices and infrastructure (e.g. data networks, computers).

### Team structure

A leading-edge digital learning strategy is likely to be implemented by multidisciplinary teams that assemble and disassemble as needed. We think that these teams in their design of learning solutions will be guided by a set of design principles, allowing for rapid development when needed. This is very different from the traditional hierarchical or matrix management structures, where the learning team, for example, would start the project, and at pre-determined project phases, request input from, or handover to, another department – e.g. marketing team for design input.

However, your organisational context will to a large extent dictate how you think about structuring the team that will support you in implementing your digital strategy. At this stage you may also want to consider the skills the team may need. If you want to implement a digital learning startegy that will truly add value to the organisation, the learning and development team cannot operate from an outdated paradigm of doing a reactive learning needs analysis and building content. From our perspective the Learning and Development practitioner will need to be able to:

- Reframe: The ability to consider a problem through different lenses. For example, a workplace safety issue can be viewed through the lens of processes, people, culture and equipment. This is very different from asking "What are your training needs?"
- Figure-it-out: This daunting emerging world of work doesn't have recipes. You will need to figure things out. This is the ability to rapidly solve problems for which there are no pre-existing answers. So, instead of seeing every problem as a nail,

and smashing it with the 'hammer' of classroom training (and Portfolio of Evidence) consider different ways and means of closing the performance gaps.

- Letting go: For this one we have a lot of sympathy as we also struggle with not wanting to control everything. This is the ability of not trying to control every aspect of the learning process because people will learn regardless of the Training Department. Rather, it is asking: How do we create the resources, infrastructure and culture so that people can learn at the point of need?

- Measure with purpose: Unfortunately most of the models we use today to measure learning are tied to the event-based model of training. This is about moving out of the narrow paradigm of measuring learning that makes measurement actually irrelevant. This is a scary place as we think we haven't found our way yet and are really unsure of how to deal with this.

## Design, delivery and governance

In this section we will provide you with a brief overview on design, delivery and governance. This is in itself a science on its own and we will merely provide an overview.

### Learning design

There is no doubt that technology can enhance the learning experience – but it should not be used as a shortcut or an excuse to abandon proper learning design principles. Your digital strategy should cater for the learning design principles and take the non-negotiables into account. Technology integration in learning can only be successful when the human element is taken into consideration. How often do we forget to ask: How do adults learn? Given our experience, we opted to improve the delivery of the learning and learner experience in order to stimulate the opportunity to learn.

Good learning design considers the mind, attitudes, behaviours, character, metacognition, and work ethics of the participant. And most importantly – time. The time to acquire and master new skills eludes many of us. People need to learn faster in the shortest time possible. So, in our view, good learning design is:

- Learner-centric (it must work for the participant – not the designer).
- Purpose driven – adults need to know the "why": Why do I need to learn this? What will I gain?
- Integrated and holistic – a seamless experience even though it may be presented in sections and modules.
- Accessible, and allows for just-in-time application. People need to be able to access what they need when they need it.
- Adult-centric – adults learn by doing and experiencing. Even though the learning is delivered through technology, it needs to encourage application and experimentation. It also needs to encourage reflection.
- Agile – allows for rapid development and rapid changes.

There will never be just one approach that you can apply in all situations, and it is very important in the field of digital learning that the principles and the science of proper instructional design are actually well understood and applied. As part of your digital strategy this is also where you consider the mix of authoring tools you may require.

A review of current authoring tools within the market

The question you need to answer here is to what extent your content approach will take into account curation, as well as creation, and how you will leverage new modalities like micro-learning and video approaches. You also need to identify new processes for digital delivery that you may need to consider. It's very important to shorten the time between identifying a learning need and meeting it. You also need to consider how you will link this approach to other approaches, e.g. classroom-based approaches, to create a seamless learner experience.

Learning assessments are important features that can support or hinder the learning experience and play a huge part in the embedment of knowledge. Creating meaningful assessments in an engaging manner is a real skill that we think is often neglected as part of the design approach.

### Learning delivery

This is your approach to the physical delivery of learning content. Here you need to consider the what, when and how of the deployment of digital learning content. This also includes your assessment approach.

Please refer back to the periodic table for the different options in terms of digital learning platforms.

### Learning governance

The concept of Corporate Governance has become increasingly important over the last decade. Legally and philosophically it is no longer acceptable for businesses to concentrate only on generating returns. This has resulted in other organisational functions also considering the impact of governance.

From our perspective learning governance is not a strategic objective. It is a systematic approach to management that enables the learning function to achieve strategic and operational objectives. It is about the processes, methods and relationships that control and direct the learning function. The following are the core components of Learning Governance:

- Appetite and approach to risk.
- Implementation of core learning management activities as set out by the learning value chain and how you will ensure effective execution over time, and enforce internal controls.
- Performance monitoring refers to the framework and metrics used to evaluate and communicate the operational effectiveness, compliance, and contribution of the learning function to business success.

From a digital learning perspective, you are faced with similar challenges to what your IT department is facing and you also need to comply with legislation in this regard. The 'viral' nature of digital learning enables information to spread rapidly and reach a wide audience. This can make it very difficult to know who has received the information or how it will spread further. Risks are inevitable and you have a moral and legal obligation to attend to the safety and well-being of your key stakeholders. You need to look at all the risks throughout the entire operation and incorporate risk management into all planning and decision-making. However, the specific focus of this section is risk management as it applies to all learning activities.

You may need to consider how you will deal with the following (and may even need to consider some formal policies and procedures):

- Global malware threats and cyber attacks.
- Enforcing the thin line between free expression by learners and inappropriate behaviours and responses.
- Plagiarism – some content is available everywhere and it is so easy to copy and paste. Have you applied all the necessary practices when you curate content or adapt it for own purposes?
- Information management – what information is required by the Learning and Development Department:

- Who, within and outside the organisation, requires access?
- Who, within and outside the organisation, needs to access and manage the information?
- How will the information be managed?
- What standards facilitate the exchange of information between internal systems and external groups?

## Measurement and business benefit realisation

The last component of your strategy is to indicate how you will know your strategy implementation is successful. You need to ask the following:

- Are we doing the right things? – Addressing the definition of the learning philosophy (philosophy and strategy building block).
- Are we doing them the right way? – Addressing the structure and the process (architecture and value chain building block).
- Are we getting them done well? – Addressing capability resource and infrastructure (design, deliver and governance building blocks).
- Are we getting the benefits? – Addressing proactive management of the process as a whole.

Please refer to chapter 5 for a detailed approach on the designing of a digital learning dashboard and more comments on learning measurements.

## Summary

The purpose of this chapter was to guide you through thinking frameworks, templates and processes on how to craft a digital learning strategy based on Chapters 1 and 2 outputs. Hopefully, this has guided and challenged your own thinking of what is a fit for purpose digital learning strategy for your own organisation.

Sadly, we have witnessed many downfalls, spent finances, and disappointment with little return for the implementation of digital learning strategies. Technology complications aside, this was often a result of not fully understanding the dynamics generated by introducing technology into the workplace, part of the lessons we have learned ourselves – the hard way. In the next chapter, we will share with how to implement your digital learning strategy and share lessons learned.

# Chapter 4

## Implementing a Digital Learning Strategy

> *"The most profound words will remain unread unless you can keep the learner engaged. You can't see their eyes to know if they got it so ... say it, show it, write it, demo it and link it to an activity."* James Bates
>
> *"Experience is what you get when you didn't get what you wanted. And experience is often the most valuable thing you have to offer."* Randy Pausch, *The Last Lecture*

## Introduction

Initially, and with a fair amount of naiveté, we thought that if you provide the infrastructure and enable people with a learning process and a logical structure, learning would just happen! Learners will learn! We even applied good adult learning principles. The metaphor that comes to mind is that in the digital learning world we tend to place people in a "classroom", put the training manual on the "table" and tell them to teach themselves.

So, we had to get smarter. We had to make explicit the learners' role and their expectations to learn outside of the "classroom". However, we all know that everyone is committed to the process in the beginning, until work and life happen – then learning is just not seen as a priority.

We have learnt that unless learning is for personal study purposes (and even the dropout rate of online degree students is high), you need to provide a clear and logical learning process. People also need to see the purpose in what they are doing – or at the very least have some sort of recognition that they have achieved something along the way. This goes way beyond the traditional structure of learning. Why must we wait until the end of the process to achieve an outcome?

Secondly, with the implementation of a digital learning strategy and the subsequent digital learning programmes it is important to consider that what you are now doing is to provide learning that is available anytime and anywhere. You are creating an organisation that is in a state of continuous learning and continuous change.

So, the purpose of this chapter is to provide:

- Some ideas and insights on getting things done – implementing your strategy.
- An approach towards learning-on boarding and digital adoption – you are asking people to learn differently.
- Sharing of some real examples and case studies of implementation of a digital strategy and approaches.

> **A Moment to Reflect**
>
> Where are some of the challenges you have faced in the past when you tried to implement your strategy? What have you learnt?

## The art of getting things done

Implementing your digital strategy will require of you to:

- Be realistic.
- Be as logical as possible.
- Ask difficult and sometimes uncomfortable questions about what you are doing, how you are doing it, and if it is delivering the results you are expecting.
- Never lose sight of the reality that in the final instance, it is the people on your team who will, or will not, get things done.
- Be deliberate in your practices.

Being deliberate in your practices includes:

1. Be clear and realistic about goals and time lines.

    Identify what is required to start executing effectively today and ensure that it is done well. Doing this consistently will allow you to gain traction on the implementation.

2. Be deliberate about the task at hand.

    It is easy to jump too far ahead, and then get distracted or disheartened. It is important to maintain discipline during execution.

3. Assess progress and refine the process.

    Step back regularly and assess whether strategic alignment and execution efforts are developing as fast and as effectively as required. Adjust practices accordingly. Allow room for failure. Assimilate methods to try things out early in the process, learn and try again.

4. Rigorous accountability.

    Strategic execution is not a once-off event. Instead, it should be seen as an ongoing responsibility and a key focus area. This is your work – the other stuff is just tools and resources.

5. Build your team.

    Make sure the right people are on board. Develop the behaviours required for success. Nurture an execution culture. Reward and celebrate execution behaviours and achievements. Be prepared to fail. Again, allow room for failure. Experimenting might mean failing sometimes. And that's okay: Sometimes the lessons learned from a failure can be more valuable than a success.

6. Make the IT department your best friend.

    It is impossible on your own to keep up with technology and the developments in this field. You will need to partner with other functions in the organisation like the IT and even marketing department.

## Learning on-boarding and a digital adoption approach

So, with the implementation of any digital strategy and digital programmes, you need to consider the learning on-boarding and digital adoption process. People need to learn differently and for Learning Departments this can be a shock because what people will learn and when they learn will be totally out of their control.

### Considerations for implementation

1. Users' level of digital skills.

    It should be no surprise that digital literacy skill is very important for effective and mindful learning in the digital learning environment.

    However, we have learned that digital learning does not have to be technology-heavy – just effective.

## Case Study: Quantum Foods

Quantum Foods is a major player in the poultry industry. Recently, times have been difficult for this industry, with avian flu causing major disruption to operations. Management wanted to focus employees attention on standardised humane culling procedures, as well as biosecurity policies and procedures.

Challenges to using digital learning as a solution included:

- Lack of computer equipment and infrastructure;
- Computer literacy levels of employees;
- Time away from work;
- National distribution footprint of farms.

The technology solution was to shoot a number of short videos presented by an experienced vet, demonstrating the correct procedures and explaining carefully the reasons why policies and procedures were mandatory. The consequences of non-compliance were also carefully discussed, so that employees started to understand the impact of their actions.

The videos were presented weekly at the start of a specified day of the week using a large television screen, and accompanied by a brief group discussion with a supervisor. Questions were answered straightaway, specific learning areas discussions were expanded upon if necessary and the best practice was reiterated. Once the video schedule was completed, the process started again.

The results were encouraging. Learners enjoyed the group learning process and the discussions were transparent. Employees who had experience in the subject matter or had seen the videos before, were happy to show that they knew why certain policies and procedures were in place. The customer felt that the intervention was a success, and is monitoring business metrics to see if the behaviour and performance of employees is making a difference to tangible outcomes.

2. Your current learning culture.

   Culture matters, immensely so. Studies have shown again and again that there may be a no more critical source of business success or failure than a company's culture – it trumps strategy and leadership. That is not to say strategy doesn't matter, but rather that the particular strategy a company employs will succeed only if it is supported by the appropriate cultural attributes.

   There is unfortunately no one best approach or a recipe that will apply in all situations that we can provide you with. Your current learning culture will either be a contributor or a hindrance to your success, and you need to adjust your implementation approach based on this.

    **Template: Analysis of current learning culture**

   - Learning is viewed as critical to improving performance
   - Learning is seen as one of the building blocks of innovation
   - Learning from taking risks is supported, mistakes aren't outright punished
   - Managers make learning part of each employee's performance goals
   - Managers actively support learning through their words and actions
   - Employees see learning as part of doing their work, not as something separate – e.g. classroom-based only
   - Managers provide feedback regularly to employees regarding progress toward learning goals
   - Peer learning is encouraged
   - Employees have opportunities to apply new learning in their jobs immediately after a learning activity
   - Feedback and self-reflection are part of the routine of all work activities
   - Managers and employees share responsibility for learning

The more questions you answer "yes" to – the stronger your learning culture. It will make the adoption of digital learning so much easier. With an understanding of the current learning culture, you can conceptualise the desired culture, which is the aspired values and key behavioural shifts, which is important in achieving the intended benefits of your digital learning strategy. A well-defined learning culture ambition provides clarity about what people do when they learn, whom they do it for, and the ways they can go about collectively reaching their goals through learning. To tap into deeper levels of motivation, individuals must feel they are contributing to something meaningful, such as making a difference to people's lives or society. The learning culture ambition must define the value it creates among the people it serves, and not merely what the culture means to the business or organisation.

3. Enablement as part of the learning process.
   It is important to understand that providing digital learning solutions doesn't necessarily mean people will just learn. Also, you need to take into account that it has to work, and work the first time. Digital learning must be simple and easy to navigate. The first time people struggle they will abandon digital learning.

4. Awareness and communication.

   We think as Learning and Development practitioners we can go and learn a couple of good lessons from the marketing department. They tell us the modern consumer says:

| You understand my circumstances and my needs | You remember what I have told you | You are always working for me | I do not need to tell you everything, you need to work out my needs |
|---|---|---|---|
| You stay out of my way until I need your help | You recognise my loyalty | You fit with my lifestyle | I trust your advice |

We don't think the modern learner differs in any way in terms of their needs and expectations. So in order to get learner engagement with our solutions, our awareness and communication campaigns need to consider these elements. Throughout the process of implementing your strategy and successfully deploying your learning solutions we recommend that you consider launching learning campaigns. Learning campaigns take on a marketing approach towards making an impact on learners. It is in essence suggesting a process and not an event. It's not just about "marketing" learning solutions to the intended audience, but using marketing concepts on content delivery itself.

5. The role of the line manager

Digital learning does not mean the coaching and sense-making role of the line manager disappears. We used to talk about our on-the-job-training approach as sit-by-Nellie. The dilemma with sit-by-Nellie is that she also teaches you her bad habits. People are predominantly social beings and making them learn in total isolation is often less effective than putting them into a classroom, despite the cost. The benefit that digital learning brings is that Nellie now provides one version of "the truth" and it serves as a reference for both the learner and the line manager.

Case Study: BMC Software, Inc.
How Hyundai used technology to create a more dynamic and inspiring learning experience

In this section we provided you with a couple of points to consider as part of your implementation approach. In the next section we will unpack this into a more practical approach by providing you with a journey roadmap.

## Learning on-boarding and digital adoption: A roadmap

David Smit[27] makes the argument that "As talent development professionals, we are very good at providing what people need to learn, and designing how they will learn, but do we do enough to explain why learning is necessary?" He further argues that if you think about how an architect designs a new building, their approach is not to build using just one type of material, but to select material appropriate to the purpose. In essence what he is saying is that Learning and Development practitioners have become learning architects who specify the various methods and modalities to build purposeful learning journeys.

This link to the purpose made us wonder how we get the modern learner to engage with learning content and to learn. As we have previously indicated, in today's work climate "learning" is often the last priority. We decided to explore the field of human motivation theories and realised that Daniel Pink's work on human motivation may hold some useful applications.

Traditionally, motivation has been seen as providing people with financial rewards that will result in increased performance and productivity. But not according to Daniel Pink.[28] Pink released his New York bestseller in 2010 entitled *Drive*. In this, Pink argues that the "carrot and stick" approach, whilst it worked in the 20th century, is not relevant to today's workforce. By combining scientific knowledge from the last 30 years with relevance to what today's businesses actually want, Pink has devised a straightforward and modern approach that can be tailored to suit an organisation's needs.

## Understanding human motivation – why would people learn?

In this section we have applied the lessons learned from the work of Daniel Pink. It is important to understand the drivers of human motivation so that we can design learning approaches and solutions that will tap into the core drivers of human motivation.

### Autonomy – provide employees with autonomy over some (or all) of their learning

In the learning world, we think this talks to the emerging trend of the personalisation of learning. This is defined as adjusting the curriculum, delivery methods and learning environment to the needs of each learner individually. Autonomy in the world of learning and development could mean:

- When they learn (time)
- How they learn (technique)
- Whom they connect with when learning (team)
- What they learn (task)

Chapter 4: Implementing a Digital Learning Strategy

## Mastery – allow employees to become better at something that matters to them

Create an environment where mastery is possible. Carefully foster a culture of learning and development by allowing for autonomy, clearly defined learning goals, immediate feedback and learning content that is challenging.

Your learning content and assessment approach needs to be challenging so that people are left with the feeling that they have accomplished something.

## Purpose – to fulfil employees' natural desire to contribute to a cause greater and more enduring than themselves

Communicate the purpose – make sure employees know and understand the purpose of learning and development as well as that of your digital learning strategy. This is about clearly understanding the why. Use purpose-oriented words – use words such as 'us' and 'we', when you implement your digital learning strategy.

Purpose is also about ensuring that learning addresses real world challenges. People want to learn that which can help them solve real-life problems, whether it is work related, personal related or that which speaks to their own personal purpose. Learning needs to be meaningful to be valuable.

*Adapted: Pink[29]*

## Asking people to learn in a new way

Do not underestimate the amount of resistance you may face from the learners themselves. If you have an organisational culture that is associated with off-site training venues and food people may resent the fact that you are replacing this with digital content. You are also asking people to learn in a new way – the responsibility for learning is moved away from the facilitator to that of the learner him or herself. This is known as self-directed learning. What we are suggesting is that your approach should consider on-boarding people to this new approach of learning prior to launching the digital learning campaigns.

## Self-directed learning

Being in the midst of a volatile and rapidly changing work environment, the motivation for identifying learning needs, locating learning resources, and the actual act of learning, needs to come from the individual. We think the self-directed learning approach will form the cornerstone of organisations that will survive and thrive in the future. This means learners need to move:

- From just following instructions to carrying out self-directed learning activities.
- From memorising and repeating to discovering, integrating, and presenting.
- From listening and reacting to communicating and taking responsibility.
- From knowledge of facts, terms, and content to understanding [and developing] processes.
- From theory to application of theory.
- From being facilitator or the Learning Department-dependent to being inter-dependent (Adapted from Intel).[30]

## How to help people become more self-directed in their learning approach

These guidelines are based on some of our own experiences as well as guidelines provided by Guglielmino[31]:

- Build an environment supportive of self-directed learning as part of your ideal learning culture.
- Promote individual awareness of self as a self-directing learner through communication and learning activities.
- Build in "transition structures" and support:

- Change learning approaches gradually, increasing learner responsibility and choices – don't opt for a "big bang" approach.
- Offer a variety of ways to demonstrate successful performance – for example, consider a gamified approach.
- Introduce problem-based learning, project-based learning, and field-based learning.
- Encourage visualisation, reflection, metacognition, and thoughtful evaluation followed by new question formation.
- Celebrate progress! Recognise success!

■ Build habits: How can we get people in the habit of learning? What habits are already in place that we can build upon?

## Digital adoption

Digital adoption, in very simple terms, refers to achieving a state within your organisation where all of your digital tools and assets are leveraged to the fullest extent. From a learning perspective this means people are utilising digital learning tools and content to their fullest. The question you need to ask as part of your digital strategy is: How will I get people to adopt the new technology and utilise it to its fullest extent? Below we will share some lessons learnt in how to increase the success rate of digital adoption.

### *Lesson 1: Leadership is key*

It is such a cliché – but our experience and the research clearly demonstrate that leadership is the single most important factor in ensuring digital adoption. Real adoption requires time and focus from the leadership.

## Case Study: Virgin Atlantic Airways—Digital Induction Programme

Virgin Atlantic is the second largest long-haul airline in the UK and the third largest European carrier over the North Atlantic. They are co-owned by the Virgin Group and Singapore Airlines. This induction programme was Virgin's first immersion into digital learning – a media-rich programme delivered through the Web.

A number of lessons was learnt – but they are emphasising the importance of involving senior management in the design of the programme, but also visibly showcasing their support for the implementation.

Adapted from: https://towardsmaturity.org/elements/uploads/Virgin_atlantic_induction.PDF

***Lesson 2: Do you know where you are going?***

*If you don't know where you are going, you might wind up someplace else.* – Yogi Berra (Famous baseball player)

The degree of success that you will have in implementing your digital learning strategy will depend on the quality and maturity of your plan. It is important that you are clear on what you are trying to achieve and why.

Chapter 4: Implementing a Digital Learning Strategy

## Case Study: The unintended consequences

A major player in the South African business sector introduced gamification and mobile learning to address the challenges faced in their organisation. The intention and the purpose of this approach was to motivate people to actually do the training and they opted for a fun and interactive way.

To their surprise people actually became quite competitive – for example, new content was deployed every Monday morning at 9:00 but not all learners were able to access this content simultaneously, resulting in some people being able to climb the leader boards more quickly. What they have learned from this is to also consider the unintended consequences of your approach. People got fixated on the gaming element and no longer on the importance of mastering the content.

### Lesson 3: Are you solving my problem?

People will not adopt digital learning if it doesn't address the skills and needs they have to address their business problems. The digital content needs to clearly match business goals and targets. Digital learning that does not support the business agenda of management and that is difficult to navigate and cumbersome will fail. Digital adoption is dependent on the ability of your content to allow for individual learners' choice and flexibility, and must be able to respond to sudden business change.

For us designing and deploying micro-learning is a good way to address this issue. It can be quickly designed in small chunks. It can be easily changed. It allows for choice.

> *The people at iSpring Solutions define micro learning as a type of learning delivered in small units. They're designed to help learners tackle a large volume of learning content by taking small chunks at a time. A micro learning course can be just a five or ten minute lesson, or a series of short stand alone lessons that are targeted on just one certain learning objective.*

### Lesson 4: Rome wasn't built in a day

We cannot overemphasise the importance of a proper strategy implementation approach. Implementation is a process and it will take time. Some common mistakes we have seen people make when implementing a digital learning strategy and/or a digital learning programme include:

- No proper change management and communication approach. You need to "sell" this to the organisation, you need to invite people to participate. Don't forget to recognise early adopters or enthusiasts that can really act as champions to your approach.

- Resistance from the Learning and Development team. If one doesn't understand nor have the necessary skills for a digital learning approach this could indeed be a daunting place. What we have also experienced are instructional designers who lack an understanding of learning processes and design issues.

- Inappropriate choices of vendors, partners and system solutions and technology.

- The devil is in the detail. Nothing leaves such a bad taste in the mouth as an implementation with errors in key administrative tasks and poorly executed systems implementation.

### Lesson 5: Less is more

We suggest that you use the simplest possible learning design and technology while still meeting the demands efficiently. In some cases, you may need advanced technology such as virtual reality, but a technology-minimalistic design will lower the risk of non-adoption. Highly sophisticated solutions that the organisation is not ready for will fail.

## It's the beginning not the end

The way we wrote this chapter may so easily create the perspective that it is done now. You have designed your digital strategy; you have successfully implemented – we can rest now. But the successful learning practitioner must prepare for the future. Technology constantly evolves, so you should stay on top of new trends in technology, new releases in platforms and tools, etc. Constantly collect feedback on user experience and digital adoption. Be proactive in mapping a journey to thrive with your current digital solution and start to make plans on how you will continue to make this better to meet business and employees' demands.

## Summary

As we said at the beginning of the chapter, we thought that if you provide the infrastructure and enable people with a learning process and a logical structure, learning would just happen. The purpose of this chapter was to share with you, the reader, lessons learnt and case studies on the implementation of a digital learning strategy. Our sincerest gratitude to the people who so selflessly allowed us to share their experiences.

The next chapter will focus on how to measure the implementation of the digital strategy and address the question on the relevance of traditional measuring models in a disruptive world. What is argued is that, learning cannot be controlled – it will happen beyond the learning department.

# Chapter 5

## Are Kirkpatrick and Phillips still relevant?

> "Not everything that counts can be counted. Not everything that is counted counts." - Einstein

## Introduction

In one of our client companies we fondly refer to their rigorous measurement practices as: "If it moves they measure it, and if it doesn't move they will kick it until it moves." This is said with good humour but it doesn't take away today's modern organisations' relentless desire to measure business value.

The measurement of digital learning strategies also appears to be a perennial topic. The issue however does not seem to be one of whether measuring the outcomes and impact of digital learning strategies is necessary (as Peter Drucker contended by saying, *"if you can't measure it, you can't manage it"*)[32], but more (1) what should be measured, (2) how, (3) what to report on to whom, and, (4) how the information generated should be used to guide a proactive learning approach that guarantees the required people capacity at the right time given future, often uncertain organisational requirements in the context of Industry 4.0.

## Modern trends in learning measurement

The modern world of learning measurement tends to not only focus on the what and how of measurement but also on analytics. Analytics in this context simply means the interpretation of data and statistics. With the abilities of the modern LMS, we see the emergence of measures linked to business outcome and a much more scientific approach to methodology and measure selection. More and more companies are looking for automated workflow to act on the data produced, and we even see the emergence of Artificial Intelligence (AI) to generate prescriptive measures.

What we are trying to address in this chapter is the question of the relevance of traditional measuring models in a disruptive world, and if those are not relevant anymore, how, then to measure the outcomes and impact of learning. What was argued in previous chapters is that learning cannot be controlled – it will happen beyond the learning department. Therefore, the questions we also need to address in this chapter if learning can't be controlled is:

1. How do we create an awareness that someone has learnt?
2. How do we track this learning?

> **A Moment to Reflect**
>
> Do you measure "learning" inside of your organisation? What works/doesn't work for you?

## Are Kirkpatrick and Phillips still relevant?

Simply, it seems to us that the purpose of measuring learning or training impact broadly has two points of departure. On the one hand there is the approach that attempts to determine to what degree development processes and programmes have some demonstrable "value". The typical and well-known approaches of Kirkpatrick and Phillips are examples of this approach. At some point in their models, both move to the second approach, which is to shift the focus away from development per se and towards the actual improvement in value added by learning or training. The following are the salient points of these two approaches:

| The Kirkpatrick four-level model typically measures: | The Phillips model measures similar constructs, namely |
|---|---|
| ■ reaction of participants – what they thought and felt about the training<br>■ learning – the resulting increase in knowledge or capability<br>■ behaviour – extent of behaviour and capability improvement and implementation/application<br>■ results – the effects on the business or environment resulting from the trainee's performance | ■ participant reaction to and satisfaction with the training programme and participants' plans for action<br>■ learning: skills and knowledge gains<br>■ application and implementation: changes in on-the-job application, behaviour change and implementation<br>■ business impact<br>■ Return on Investment (ROI): compares the monetary value of the business outcomes with the costs of the training programme |

It seems to us that the inherent assumptions of both approaches can be summarised as follows:

- It measures training impact.
- It is evaluating everything after the fact.
- The unit of measure remains individual skill.
- It assumes a direct relationship between skills acquired and job/organisation impact and masks the reality of transfer of training efforts into measurable results.

These models essentially attempt to isolate training or learning efforts from the systems, context, and culture in which the learner operates. What we are further arguing is that in a digital world these traditional models do not sufficiently answer all the questions: (1) what should be measured, (2) how, (3) what to report on to whom, and, (4) how the information generated should be used to guide a proactive learning approach. Therefore, in the next sections we will attempt to provide you with a practical model on how to answer these questions for your business.

## It starts with why

As previously mentioned Learning and Development practitioners don't usually debate whether It is necessary to measure, but the questions are more related to what and how. But before we answer those, let's just consider the why of measurement. Until you have clarified the why in your own head it will remain a daunting and uncomfortable exercise.

> **Personal Reflection**
>
> Personally I use to hate all kinds of conversations about learning measurement. I always thought it was a way to proof my reason for existence within the organisation, and I thought if line managers can't see the value learning and development adds they shouldn't be in that position.
>
> It took me a long time to figure out that was not the reason to measure, for me my "hate" relationship with measurement changed the day when I figured out the why.

For us some of the why lies in the ability to make sense of people performance and our ability to explain these trends. It is so that we can offer the best fit for purpose solutions for our organisations. It is to know do we actually add value, for whom and what do they perceive as valuable. This allows us to perform better and to focus on doing the right things right.

If you cannot answer the so-what question you maybe need to consider why you are measuring at all.

## What should be measured – the Digital Learning Dashboard

The next question we need to answer is the what we want to measure. Various frameworks exist but we think the Digital Learning Dashboard should at least consider measuring:

- Planning and design, meaning did we get the input requirements right, and was the learning strategy, process, approach/interventions and delivery methodology fit-for-purpose?
- The success of implementation of learning interventions, meaning did the right people learn what they were supposed to?
- The outcomes thereof IN the business, meaning, did the application of learning (new knowledge, skills, behaviours) indeed improve individual and/or team performance?
- The impact thereof ON the business, meaning did it indeed realise the business benefits intended to ensure the success of the organisation over the longer term? For example, the fact that we are known in the industry for the quality of learning offering – does that increase our ability to attract the right talent?

For a digital learning dashboard, you may want to consider the following conceptual view:

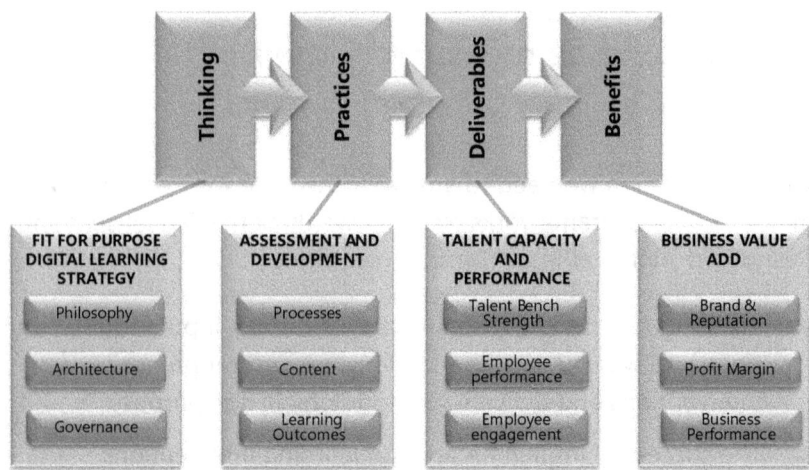

*Figure 5.1: A possible digital learning dashboard*

None of the above sounds particularly new, novel or earth shattering. Yet surprisingly, not many businesses we engage with seem to do this in a deliberate or thoughtful manner. Those that do, more often than not, fall into the trap of assuming that measures of business or people outcomes or value add are a single set of metrics. We call this a trap because not only should measures be grouped as indicated above, but they could also be levelled as the example below illustrates:

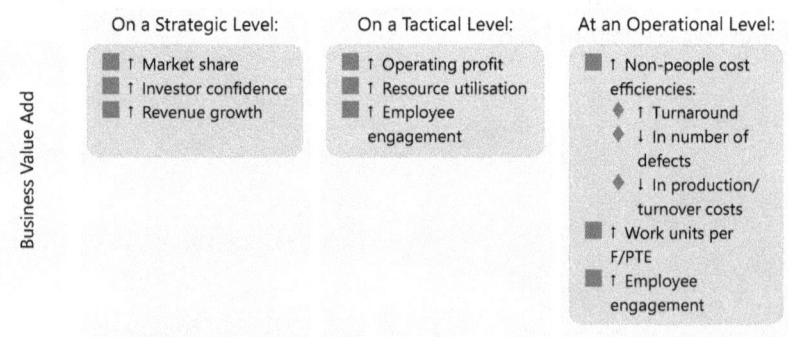

*Figure 5.2: A levelled approach to measurement*

What is very important when you consider putting together your conceptual digital learning dashboard is:

- Whatever it is that you do and deliver, must lead to demonstrable business value-added impact.

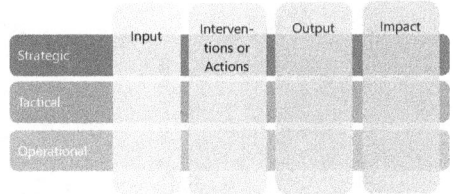

- In order for something to add value, you have to ensure that the right outputs/outcomes are delivered.

- This means that digital learning interventions/actions must be relevant to the intended outputs/outcomes to address specific business issues – the business problems/opportunities you are addressing through the digital learning strategy.

What you will see is that we are now considering measures of:

- Efficiency
- Effectiveness
- Outcome or Impact

and more importantly, we are not only measuring a specific learning event like a sales training programme, but we are measuring the impact of how we think of learning and development, our practices and approaches and our learning programmes.

So, if we apply this logic to our conceptual dashboard design, the following picture may emerge:

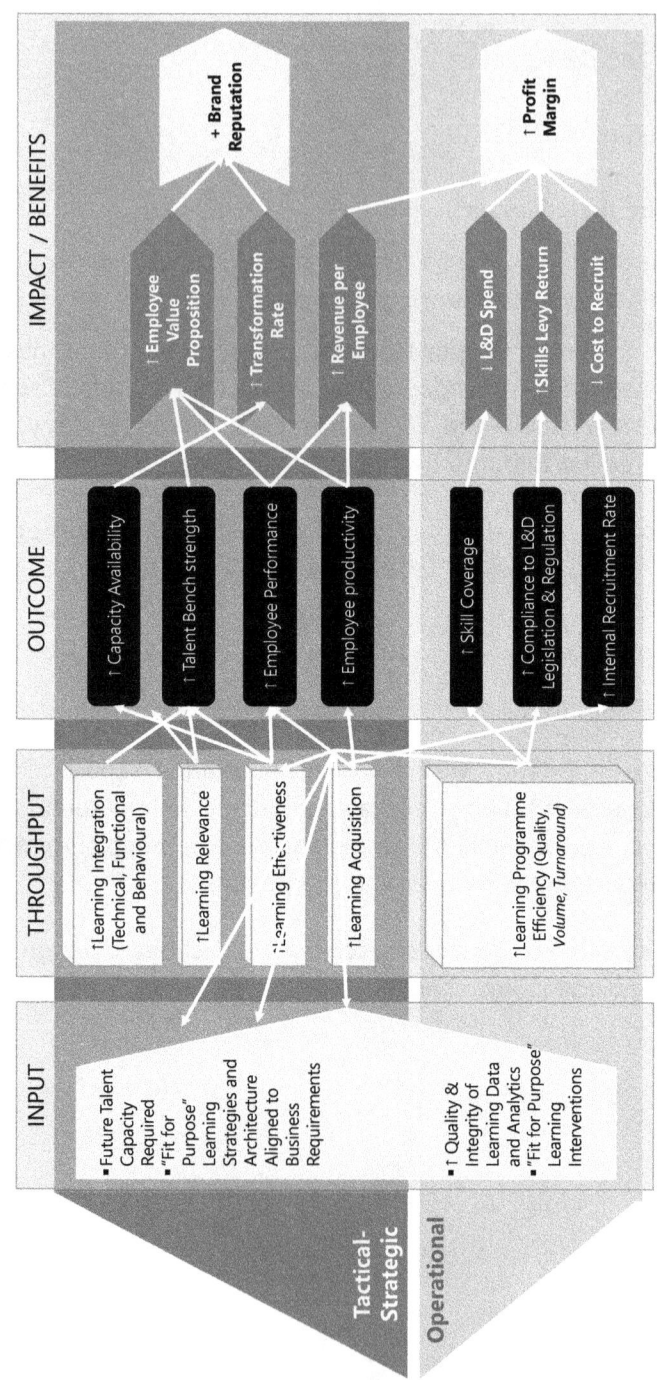

*Figure 5.3: An extended view of a digital learning dashboard*

## How should it be measured – Learning Analytics and Tools

Before we unpack the process regarding how it should be measured, we will start this section off by just clarifying some terminology.

- **Measure:** A measure defines "what" needs to be measured, meaning the actual indicator that will show progress or performance, i.e. employee productivity.
- **Metric:** The metric describes how the measure will be measured and is often defined as a type of formula or calculation, i.e. employee productivity (measure) can be measured by calculating the number of units delivered per individual in a given timeframe (metric). The metric should provide the "proof" of a measure to be interpreted as positive or negative.
- **Analytics:** Analytics are typically the outcome of comparing/combining/statistically analysing/trending etc. various metrics, and provide data or statistics for interpretation.

### Design the logical dashboard

The design of the Logical Model refers to the process through which to:

1. **Determine the "proof"** – thus, the actual measures and metrics, the relationship between these measure relationships, units of measurement, source data etc. This is done through a collaborative process with various organisational stakeholders (typically operations, finance, human capital and IT) to ensure that it is "SMART" (specific, measurable, achievable, realistic and time-targeted).

2. **Confirm the "how" and "when"**, meaning the methods, applications and tools for measurement. The measuring methods may be quantitative, qualitative or combined, and the tools may be manual or automated (preferably automated).

Overall, it is important that the methods, tools and people are directly aligned to what is being measured, as well as the indicators or "proof" for each measure.

## Examples of digital measures and metrics

To get you started below are examples of questions you may want to consider when you decide on your measures and metrics. Just remember, in the context of measurement less is more. Don't fall into the trap of having measurements for the sake of measurement. Go back to the answers to your why question – why are you measuring?

|  | **Throughput** | **Outcome** | **Impact** |
|---|---|---|---|
| **Tactical-Strategic** | ■ Is our learning strategy relevant and does it address the organisational needs?<br><br>■ How well do we help our colleagues build the competence and expertise they need most?<br><br>■ How well do we manage internal learning, governance and risk? | ■ Are our employees engaged?<br>– levels of engagement<br><br>■ Are we able to recruit for key positions from within?<br>– number of positions filled internally/number of positions available<br><br>■ What are the efficiency and effectiveness levels of our development processes?<br><br>■ How well are we using our investments and resources?<br><br>■ Does learning strengthen the overall wellness of the organisation? | ■ What are stakeholder perceptions regarding our ability to people capacity?<br><br>■ What is the rate of innovation in the organisation and in which way did we contribute? |

## Chapter 5: Are Kirkpatrick and Phillips still relevant?

|  | Throughput | Outcome | Impact |
|---|---|---|---|
| **Operational** | ■ Are our learning programmes aligned to business demands and needs?<br><br>■ To what extent does our digital learning content allow for transfer back into the workplace?<br><br>■ How rapidly can we design, deploy and scale programmes? | ■ What did the learner think of the learning experience?<br>– learner satisfaction<br>– abandonment rate<br><br>■ What did the learner learn (new level of proficiency)?<br>– competence pre- and post<br>– progress and completion rates<br><br>■ What is the rate of digital learning share; do people share knowledge and skills?<br><br>■ To what extent are people using our performance support tools? | ■ What are our customer satisfaction results saying?<br><br>■ What is our current digital adoption rate?<br><br>■ What are our key business performance indicators saying – e.g. productivity, safety<br><br>■ How well do we help our colleagues to achieve peak performance? |

Good measures have three properties: universality, uniformity, and reliability. Uniformity means the measure is interpreted the same way in all contexts; universality means it applies to all relevant entities; and reliability means that its predictions confirm what theory says should happen.

## Template: Measure and Metric

| Measure | Purpose | Metric: Competence Rate | | | | |
|---|---|---|---|---|---|---|
| | | Unit of Measurement | Frequency | Link(s) | Data source/ Tool | Indicator |
| What did people learn | Measure of Effectiveness | 5-point scale | 3 months after programme completion | Impact measures on safety culture | LMS | % improvement |
| | | Metric: Learner Perception | | | | |
| | | Unit of Measurement | Frequency | Link(s) | Data source/ Tool | Indicator |
| | | % favourable | After programme completion | Programme design and content measures | Survey/ Programme evaluation forms | Target of 80% |

| Measure | Purpose | Metric: Workplace application | | | | |
|---|---|---|---|---|---|---|
| | | Unit of Measurement | Frequency | Link(s) | Data source/ Tool | Indicator |
| Productivity improvement | Measure of Impact | % who applied | Every 6 months | Programme alignment to business needs | Survey | 70% target |
| | | Metric: Performance rating | | | | |
| | | Unit of Measurement | Frequency | Link(s) | Data source/ Tool | Indicator |
| | | % improvement | Every 6 months | Programme design and content measures | Performance management system | 5% improvement target |

## Design the physical dashboard or scorecard

The design of the Physical Model refers to the process through which to develop the actual tools to gather and collate data and information. This will include defining the processes that should be followed to convert data from the source to the final dashboards, building the data warehouses, and loading information onto them, what would be preferred, an automated Management and Performance system. To complete this phase, you will need to collaborate with the Information Technology and Business Intelligence teams. As previously mentioned – make sure IT is your best friend.

## Measurement we can't control

Traditionally, the learning or training department had a purpose for existence – the design and implementation of formal development solutions. The reality is that people learn everywhere – in both formal and informal environments – in the lifts up to their offices, on their smoke breaks and coffee runs, in team meetings, while being coached, while reading, while surfing the internet, on training courses and in multiple other circumstances.

So, learning cannot be controlled – it will happen beyond the learning department. So how do we track learning in a digital age where is doesn't necessarily fall within our area of control? Some of our initial thinking here is that we need to extend our tracking mechanisms to monitor progress, scores and completion of compatible courses on an LMS to the Experience API (xAPI).

For those readers interested (some may find this too technical and you are welcome to skip to the next lesson), the theory behind xAPI is that it will enable learners to log all the learning they are exposed to, whatever the circumstances. It is aimed at ensuring that all this continuous development is logged and tracked.

Conceptually, it can look like this:

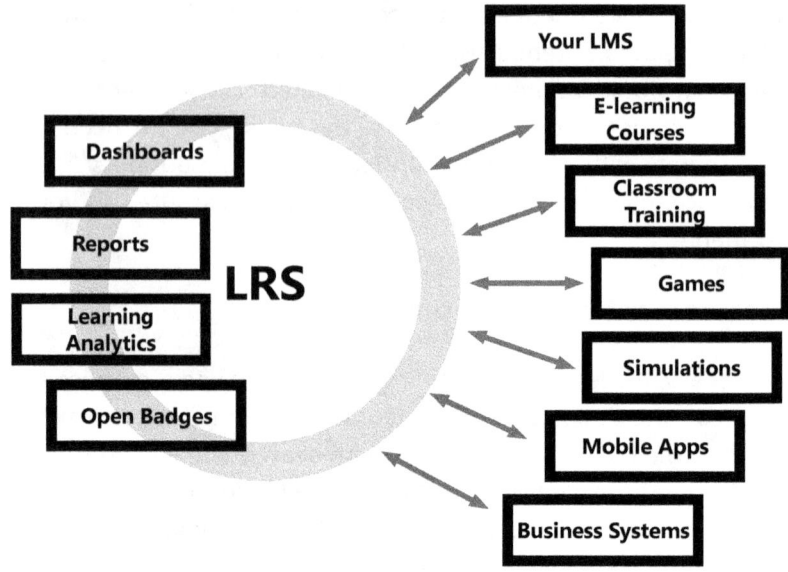

*Figure 10: The experience API ecosystem*[33]

From this picture, you can see the Learning Record Store (LRS) stores data about learning experiences from a range of sources, known as Activity Providers (any tool or system that generates data about learning experiences, achievements and job performance). The LRS uses this data in dashboards, reports, learning analytics and can even award Open Badges. It also makes the data available for other systems to use. The diagram shows the LRS as a stand-alone system, but the LRS is most likely already incorporated into your current LMS.

It all seems logical – we completely subscribe to the premise – but then, what systems are being utilised to capture the experience? How are people logging what they have done? The idea of systems spitting out xAPI statements is appealing, but it presupposes that systems are designed with this in mind. Maybe a better way of doing this is for people to capture experiences on specific mobile apps, which incorporate the custom statements which describe what they have done.

In essence, what we are saying is that the technology exists and it can do so much, but that is not the point. Be careful to not be seduced by the technology, be clear when you define your digital learning strategy and measurement approach on why, what and how and the readiness of your own organisation. An organisation without a learning culture will find implementing these kind of initiatives a lot more difficult to do.

Experience API (xAPI) – The Ultimate Guide

All you need to know and how it works

A collection of Experience API (xAPI) Case Studies

## Negative effects of measurement

Through the years what we have learnt when putting measures and metrics together is that they often have some unintended consequences. According to Heesen[34] some of the most relevant, unintended, negative effects of measurement are:

- Tunnel vision: Focusing on what is easy to measure instead of what is important.
- Measure fixation: Trying to change definitions to make the numbers look better.
- Misrepresentation: Cheating the system.
- Ossification: Presenting outdated information.

- Gaming: Underachieving, once targets have been made.
- Misinterpretation: Incorrect or incomplete interpretation of the metrics.
- Sub-optimisation: Using corporate resources to optimise one's own targets, instead of corporate objectives.
- Myopia: Focusing on the short-term quick wins, instead of longer-term strategic objectives of your digital strategy.

We spoke about unintended consequences previously – have you considered the negative effects of your measurement approach?

## Summary

Figure 5.4 below summarises the process of designing and implementing a learning dashboard. As this book focuses on digital learning, we in this chapter focused more on the measures of digital learning. However, we think that if you have the need to actually go beyond just a conceptual model, the dashboard will need to focus on your entire learning and even talent strategy. The same principles will apply though.

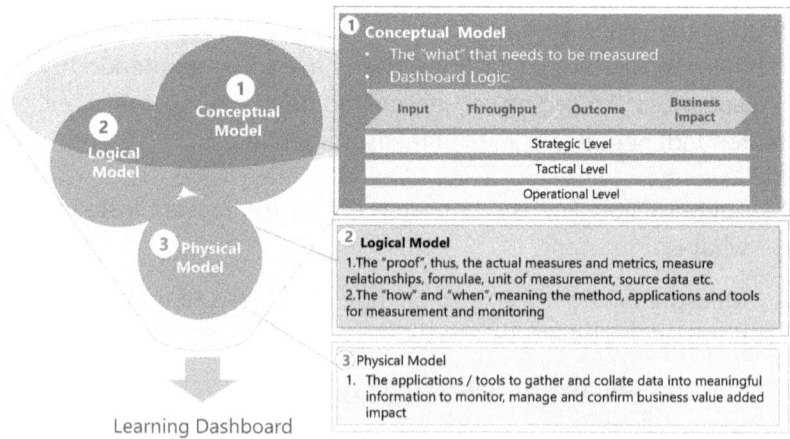

Figure 5.4: The phases of designing a digital learning dashboard

## What should be reported on to whom and the decisions to be made – Learning Reporting Framework

*"If a measurement matters at all, it is because it must have some conceivable effect on decisions and behaviour. If we can't identify a decision that could be affected by a proposed measurement and how it could change those decisions, then the measurement simply has no value."* - Douglas W. Hubbard

Ultimately the purpose of measurement is to inform decision making. So in this final section we will unpack what to do with the information contained in your dashboard. News Media Consortium[35] defines learning analytics as *"...education's approach to 'big data', a science that was originally leveraged by businesses to analyze commercial activities, identify spending trends, and predict consumer behavior. Education is embarking on a similar pursuit into data science with the aim of improving student retention and providing a high quality, personalized experience for learners. Learning analytics research uses data analysis to inform decisions made on every tier of the educational system. This data can be leveraged to build better pedagogies and target at-risk learners."*

Learning analytics has emerged as one of the most common terms for Learning and Development practitioners seeking to understand the implications of Big Data and Businesses Intelligence on how they analyse learning data, and improve learning systems through evidence-based adoption.

> Very simple but **big data** is larger, more complex data sets that are so voluminous that traditional data processing software just can't manage it. However, it does create the option to address business problems which wasn't possible in the past.

In this section we will provide you with a number of possible reporting frameworks on how to report on the progress of your digital learning strategy implementation as well as measuring the impact of digital learning solutions.

Your reporting framework here will cater for:

- Descriptive Analytics, which use data aggregation and data mining to provide insight into the past and answer: "What has happened?"
- Predictive Analytics, which use statistical models and forecast techniques to understand the future and answer: "What could happen?"
- Prescriptive Analytics, which use optimisation and simulation algorithms to advise on possible outcomes and answer: "What should we do?"

(source: Halo Business Intelligence.[36]

## Reporting Framework: Whom

An important question to consider when you report any information on your digital learning dashboard is to consider who needs to know this, why they need to know this and what do you want them to do with the information.

Chapter 5: Are Kirkpatrick and Phillips still relevant?

**Template: Stakeholder Groupings**

| | Stakeholder Grouping | | | |
|---|---|---|---|---|
| | **Operations Executives** | **Operations Management** | **Talent Management Executives** | **Talent Management Professionals** |
| **What do they want to know** | Are we executing on business strategy?<br><br>Are we mitigating business risks? | Are we meeting operational targets?<br><br>Is the time spend on training worth it?<br><br>Are we operational efficient? | How are we supporting the business strategy?<br><br>Do we have the right talent for now and the future? | Is the team meeting targets?<br><br>How can I improve my training programme? |
| **What must they do with information I shared** | | | | |

If you cannot answer the what must they do with the information (e.g. make improvements) then you may need to re-consider why you are reporting on this. The exception is when you want to just indicate progress and don't necessarily want people to respond to the information shared.

You may also want to consider:

- Are these audiences currently using reports, for what purposes, and what is missing from them?
- Have they asked for information?
- Are you confident that the data/information you provide to them will actually be understood and that they will know how to respond to the information?
- To what extent are they data and information literate?

## Reporting Framework: Information about the strategy execution

In the section below we will provide some examples of what you can consider reporting on from the strategy execution perspective. The questions as previously alluded to that you want answered:

- Are we doing the right things? – Addressing the definition of the learning philosophy (philosophy and strategy building block).
- Are we doing them the right way? – Addressing the structure and the process (architecture and value chain building block).
- Are we getting them done well? – Addressing capability resource and infrastructure (design, deliver and governance building blocks).
- Are we getting the benefits? – Addressing proactive management of the process as a whole.

Below are some examples you may want to consider.

*Answering questions about what has happened*

**Example**: Progress against your identified goals and budget management. Feedback on resource utilisation, team growth etc.

*Answering questions about what could happen*

**Example:** This could include the identified risks and your mitigation strategies.

*Answering questions about what should we do*

**Example**: The extent to which the digital strategy is still relevant in terms of business requirements and what should/could be changed.

## Reporting Framework: Information about the learner and the learner experience

If you currently have a learning platform in place (and depending on the type of LMS) you may encounter analytics in the dashboard section. This is essentially as a result of the impact of Business Intelligence products on learning platforms. You may want to consider using some of those analytics if appropriate.

*Answering questions about what has happened*

**Example:** Think about basic arithmetic like sums, averages, percent changes. Compiling information about learner completion rate, abandonment rate, etc. This information is often required from a compliance reporting perspective.

*Answering questions about what could happen*

**Example:** Tracking learner performance will give you a sense of which learners are at risk of not mastering the skill or content. Identifying these individuals early in the process allows for preventative measures.

*Answering questions about what should we do*

**Example**: Analysing data on how long learners are interacting with the content (e.g. video, articles) will help you see how engaging the content is and how well the method of delivery is in creating understanding of the subject matter.

**Example**: Using polling as part of the virtual classroom experience can show how comfortable learners are with the material as it is being facilitated and can help facilitators make the necessary adjustments to better align methods and techniques.

## Reporting Framework: Information about business impact

This will be a function of your organisational context and what is important to whom. Here we suggest:

- Compile a list of key stakeholders.
- Define what impact measures could be important to them e.g. you may want to ask what the benefits of the digital learning strategy are for them.
- Report in terms of what happened, what could happen, what we should do.

Examples of benefits could include:

- Benefits that mean customers' requirements can be responded to in an improved way.
- Benefits relating to the improvement in decision-making or other internal processes.
- Benefits that contribute to an improvement in employee engagement and productivity.
- Benefits that enable the execution of the organisation's strategy.
- Benefits relating to improved revenue and margins.

## Creating a culture of measurement

For a lot of Learning and Development practitioners the measurement of learning is daunting and we tend to be afraid of it. Below are a couple of suggestions you may want to consider to get rid of this fear of measurement:

- It starts with the belief that measurement is a valuable process and it can add benefits to the business; it is not a way to justify the existence of the learning department.
- Take your stance on measurement, be clear on why, what and how you will measure.

- Build in recognition and rewards processes in your own team to drive a culture of measurement.
- Remove barriers to measurement.
- Build data and information literacy if necessary.

## Storytelling with Data

Ever forced to sit through a presentation where the numbers and the graphs were just thrown at you? We think that numbers alone – even those that are viewed as mission critical – are meaningless unless you are able to create context and tell the story. Stephen Few provided some practical advice on how to tell some compelling stories with the stats.

A Statistical Narrative – Telling Compelling Stories with Numbers

## Summary

 Application of this approach is different from a typical ROI approach, both philosophically and practically. Building such an approach takes time and it requires conversations to create alignment on the learning philosophy, adjustment of learning practices to drive integration and to ensure consistency of all other people and talent-management practices.

It requires the learning and development executive to take a perspective on:

- Context – business brand, strategy, external strategic drivers.

- Purpose – specific advantages to be achieved through digital learning excellence.
- Process – specific processes of design, development and assessment.
- Content – ensure that all content and assessment plugged into processes are fit for purpose.

It is a lot of hard work, but reporting from a business benefit perspective does provide a powerful way to make better decisions concerning digital learning excellence. It allows you to respond timeously and rapidly to challenges.

# References

1. Nzimande, B. (2013). Department of Labour (DoL) Employment Equity (EE) and Transformation Indaba gala dinner last night (April 18). Retrieved from: https://www.labourguide.co.za/latest-news-1/1616-billions-spent-on-training-but-the-investment-has-not-advanced-transformation-departments-transformation-indaba-told
2. LinkedIn Learning. (2018). 2018 Workplace Learning Report: The Rise and Responsibility of Talent Development in the New Labor Market. Retrieved from: https://learning.linkedin.com/resources/workplace-learning-report-2018
3. Bersin, J. (2018). A New Paradigm for Corporate Training: Learning in the Flow of Work. Retrieved from: https://joshbersin.com/2018/06/a-new-paradigm-for-corporate-training-learning-in-the-flow-of-work/
4. Ibid.
5. Pankin, J., Roberts, J. & Savio, M. (2012). Blended Learning at MIT. Retrieved from: http://web.mit.edu/training/trainers/resources/blended_learning_at_mit.pdf
6. Bersin, 2018.
7. Bunchball. (2007). Why Bunchball? Retrieved from: https://www.bunchball.com/about/why-bunchball
8. Goldman, S.L., Nagel R.N. & Preis, K. (1994). *Agile Competitors and Virtual Organizations: Strategies for Enriching the Customer*. New York: Wiley.
9. Howard, L. (2015). What Does it Mean to Have an Agile Mindset. Retrieved from: https://www.agileconnection.com/article/what-does-it-mean-have-agile-mindset?
10. Bersin, 2018.
11. Bersin, J. (2019). Corporate Learning 2019: Three Things to Remember. Retrieved from: https://www.youtube.com/watch?v=L7gOIvtJvBo
12. Bower, J.L. and Christensen, C.M. (1995). Disruptive technologies – catching the wave. *Harvard Business Review*, 73 (1), Jan-Feb: pp.43-53.
13. Bersin, 2019.
14. Bersin, 2018.
15. Rouse, M. (2018). The essential guide to managing HR technology trends: AI (artificial intelligence). Retrieved from: https://searchenterpriseai.techtarget.com/definition/AI-Artificial-Intelligence

16  Kamasheva, A.V., Valeev, E.R., Yagudin, R.Kh. and Maksimova, K.R. (2015). Usage of Gamification Theory for Increase Motivation of Employees. *Mediterranean Journal of Social Sciences*, Vol 6(1 S3). Retrieved from: https://www.mcser.org/journal/index.php/mjss/article/download/5674/5470

17  Gutierrex, K. (2014). Getting Buy-In for eLearning: A 3-Step Process. Retrieved from: https://www.shiftelearning.com/blog/bid/345991/Getting-Buy-In-for-eLearning-A-3-Step-Process

18  Evans, D. (2013). eLearning Success – measuring the ROI impact and benefits. eLearning What's Next? Retrieved from: http://www.theinformationdaily.com/2013/05/10/e-learning-success-measuring-the-roi-impact-andbenefits

19  Deloitte Development LLC. (n.d.). Leading in Learning: Building capabilities to deliver on your business strategy. Retrieved from: https://www2.deloitte.com/content/dam/Deloitte/global/Documents/HumanCapital/gx-cons-hc-learning-solutions-placemat.pdf

20  World Economic Forum. (2016). The Future of Jobs. Retrieved from: http://reports.weforum.org/future-of-jobs-2016/

21  Institute for the Future. (2011). The Re-working of "Work". Retrieved from: http://www.iftf.org/futureworkskills/

22  Study.com. (n.d.). The Emperor's New Clothes: Summary & Moral. Retrieved from: https://study.com/academy/lesson/the-emperors-new-clothes-summary-moral.html

23  Cuban, L. (2015), "Larry Cuban on school reform and classroom practice: the lack of evidence-based practice: the case of classroom technology", Retrieved from: https://larrycuban.wordpress.com/2015/02/05/the-lack-of-evidence-based-practice-the-case-of-classroom-technology-part-1/

24  Deloitte. (2019). Learning in the flow of life: 2019 Global Human Capital Trends. Retrieved from: https://www2.deloitte.com/za/en/pages/human-capital/articles/learning-in-the-flow-of-life.html

25  Pankin, Roberts & Savio. (2012).

26  Pearce II, J.A. & Robinson Jr, R.B. (2003). *Strategic management: Formulation, Implementation and Control.* Eighth edition. New York: McGraw-Hill, Inc., p137.

27  Smit, D. (2018). *To Engage the Modern Learner, Start With Why.* https://www.td.org/insights/to-engage-the-modern-learner-start-with-why

28  Pink, D.H. (2010). *Drive: The Surprising Truth. About What Motivates us.* New York: Riverhead Books.

29  Ibid.

30. INTEL. 2003. Teach to the future. Project-based classroom: Bridging the gap between education and technology. [Training materials for regional and master trainers].
31. Guglielmino, L.M. (2013). The Case for Promoting Self-Directed Learning in Formal Educational Institution. *SA-eDUC Journal,* Vol 10(2).
32. Peter Drucker, "The New Productivity Challenge," *Harvard Business Review*, (November-December 1991): 70.
33. Rustici Software LLC. (2019). The Enterprise Learning Ecosystem. Retrieved from: https://xapi.com/ecosystem/
34. Heesen, B. (2015). Effective Strategy Execution: Improving Performance with Business Intelligence. Retrieved from: https://www.springer.com/gp/book/9783662479223
35. Digital Learning Toolkit. (2017). Learning Analytics. Retrieved from: https://dltoolkit.mit.edu/online-course-design-guide/evaluation/learning-analytics/
36. Halo Business Intelligence. (2019). Descriptive, Predictive, and Prescriptive Analytics Explained. Retrieved from: https://halobi.com/blog/descriptive-predictive-and-prescriptive-analytics-explained/

# Index

## A

agile content development, 57
agility/flexibility, 55
agile organisation, 2, 8
applications and tools, 17, 24, 91, 98
approach to measurement, 88
apps for learning practitioners, 28
architecture and value chain, 54, 63, 102
art of getting things done, 67
artificial intelligence, 2, 17, 25, 84
assessment tools, 17, 27

## B

being of agile, 9
business problems/opportunities, 49, 89
business systems, 96

## C

challenge of recalling information, 37
classroom training, 7, 59, 96
collaborative learning, 34, 37, 91
content curation, 29
content platforms, 18
creating a culture of measurement, 104
current paradigm, 10–11

## D

dashboards, 95–96
delivery and governance, 59
demanding and on-demand, 37
design a digital learning strategy, 43–64
design approach, 31, 61, 74
design content, 17, 24
design criteria, 54
design e-learning/online, 30
design methodologies, 17, 28
design mind-set, 41
design of learning curriculums, 56
design principles, 30, 54, 58
proper learning, 30, 59
design programmes, 30
digital learning dashboard, 63, 87–88, 90, 98, 100
digital learning infrastructure, 18
Digital Learning Strategy, 43, 54, 65, 81
digital learning value chain, 55–56
digital measures and metrics, 92
digital myths, 31
disruption, 15, 41, 69

# Index

doing of agile, 9

## E

experience API ecosystem, 96

## G

games, 5, 96
gamification, 7, 16, 22, 26, 79

## I

implementation, 2, 19, 57, 62–64, 66–68, 70, 73, 78, 80–81, 85, 87, 95, 100
implementing a digital learning strategy, 65, 80
industry and internal dynamics, 46–47
information about business impact, 104
information about the learner and the learner experience, 103
information about the strategy execution, 102
infrastructure, 17–18, 56, 58–59, 63, 65, 69, 81, 102
interfaces and the Cloud, 23

## L

leadership is key, 77
learn in a new way, 75

learning analytics, 12, 91, 96, 99
learning analytics and tools, 91
learning and development, 1–4, 8, 10–11, 13–16, 34, 38, 41, 45–46, 48–54, 58, 71, 73–75, 86, 89, 104–105
learning and development landscape, 1, 45–46
learning approach, 31, 49, 76, 80, 83, 86
learning architecture, 52, 54
learning culture, 49–50, 52–53, 70–71, 76, 97
learning delivery, 61
learning design, 19, 30–31, 50, 59–60, 80
learning governance, 61
learning on-boarding, 56, 68, 73
learning on-boarding and a digital adoption approach, 68
learning philosophy, 7, 46, 48–49, 53–54, 57, 63, 102, 105
learning philosophy and strategy, 48, 54, 57
learning reporting framework, 99
learning, self-directed, 75–76
logical dashboard, 91

## M

measurement, 59, 63, 83–84, 86, 88, 91–92, 94–95, 97–99, 104–105

measurement and business benefit realisation, 63
mobile apps, 96
modern learner, 34–37, 40–41, 47–48, 72–73
modern trends in learning measurement, 84
multi-generational learning, 38

## N

negative effects of measurement, 97

## O

organisation as a machine, 2–3

## P

past, the present and the future, 1, 14
periodic table of digital learning, 17
phases of designing a digital learning dashboard, 98
physical dashboard, 94
programme delivery platforms, 18, 21

## R

regulatory environment, 46–47
reporting framework, 99–100, 102–104
roadmap, 73

## S

self-directed learning, 75–76
simulations, 23, 27, 96
storytelling with data, 105
strategic objectives, 53–54, 98

## T

team structure, 58
technology architecture, 56–57
thinking framework, 45
training, 1–7, 10, 12, 25, 30, 35–37, 51–52, 58–59, 72, 75, 79, 84–86, 89, 95–96, 101

## U

understanding human motivation, 74
unpacking the environment, 47

## W

workflow learning tools, 17, 24

www.ingramcontent.com/pod-product-compliance
Lightning Source LLC
Chambersburg PA
CBHW071624170426
43195CB00038B/2106